Yosemite's Forgotten Pioneers

Yosemite's Forgotten Pioneers

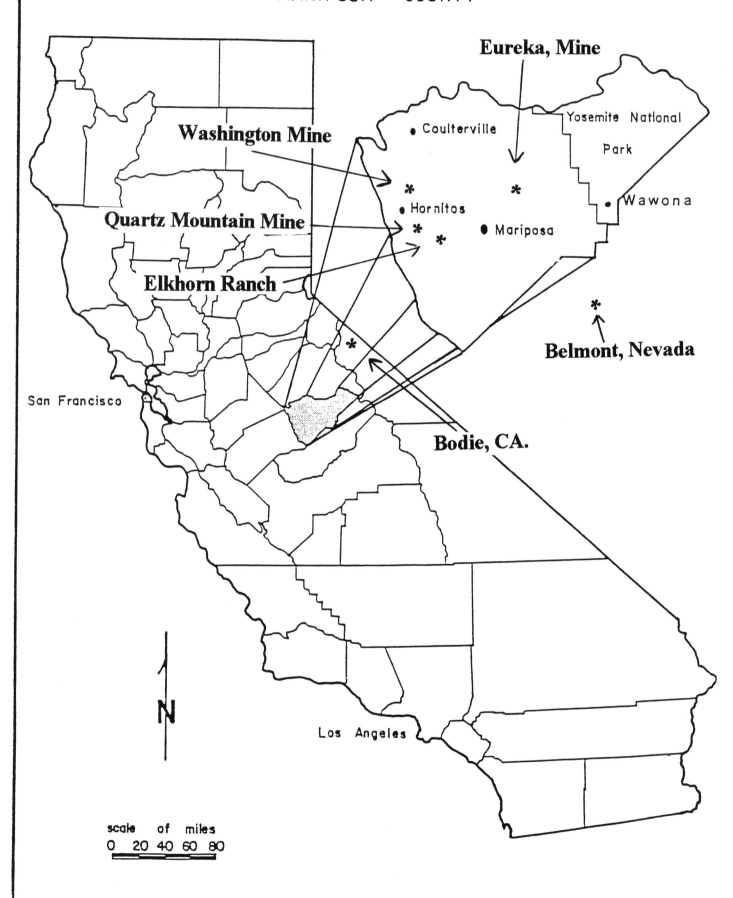

LOCATION OF
MARIPOSA COUNTY

Eureka, Mine

Washington Mine

Quartz Mountain Mine

Elkhorn Ranch

Coulterville

Yosemite National
Park

Wawona

Hornitos

Mariposa

Belmont, Nevada

San Francisco

Bodie, CA.

Los Angeles

N

scale of miles
0 20 40 60 80

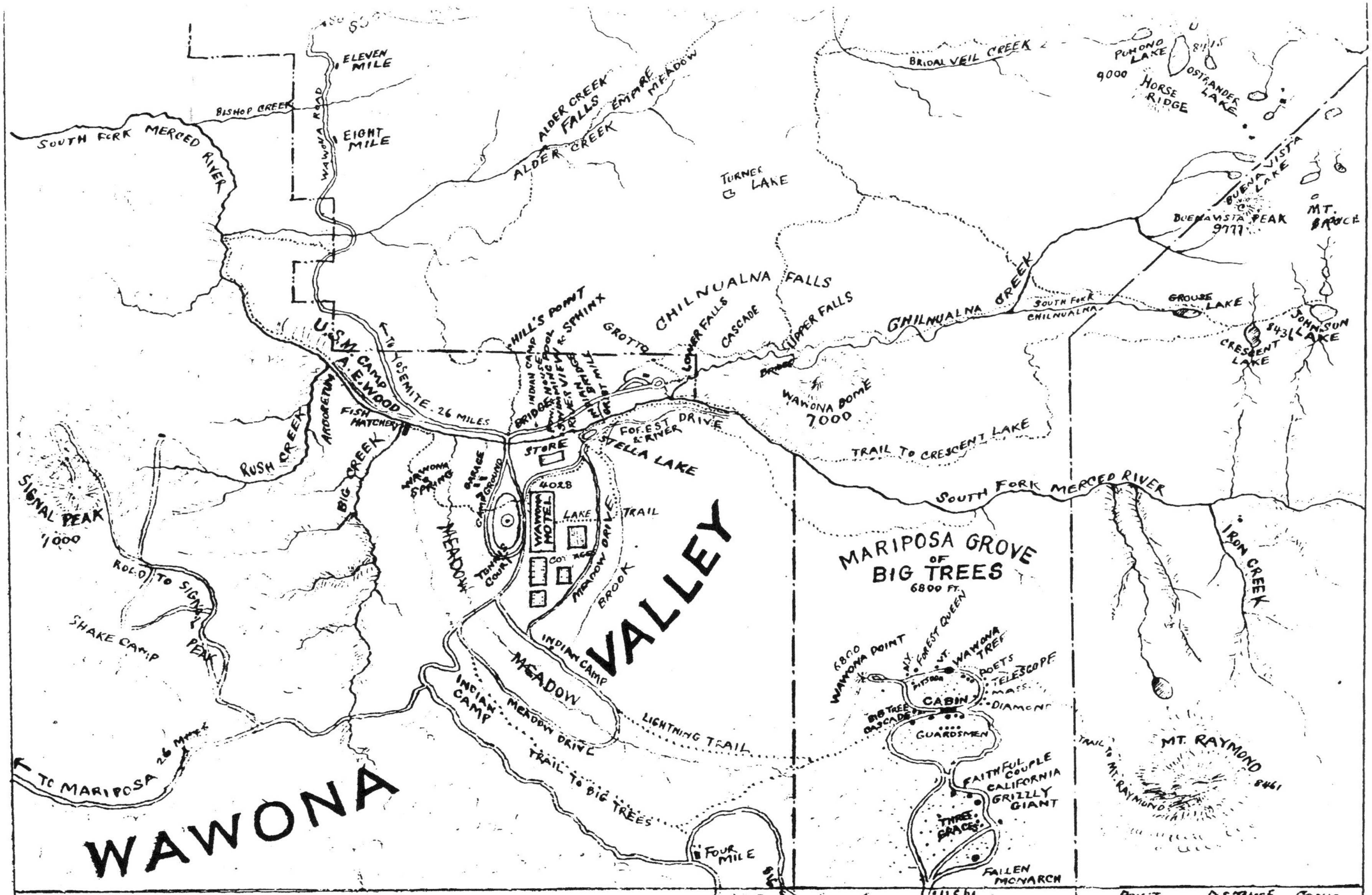

WAWONA

POINTS OF INTEREST ABOUT WAWONA

WAWONA SECTION
DRAWN BY ROGT. R. HILL

Map labels (place names and features):

- SOUTH FORK MERCED RIVER
- BISHOP CREEK
- WAWONA ROAD
- ELEVEN MILE
- EIGHT MILE
- BRIDAL VEIL CREEK
- HORSE RIDGE
- PUNDRO LAKE 9000
- OSTRANDER LAKE
- MT. BRUCE
- BUENA VISTA PEAK 9777
- JOHNSUM LAKE
- CRESCENT LAKE
- GROUSE LAKE
- IRON CREEK
- MT RAYMOND 8641
- TRAIL TO MT. RAYMOND
- SOUTH FORK MERCED RIVER
- CHILNUALNA CREEK
- SOUTH FORK CHILNUALNA
- CHILNUALNA FALLS
- UPPER FALLS
- CASCADE
- LOWER FALLS
- CHILNUALNA FALLS
- TURNER LAKE
- WAWONA DOME 7000
- TRAIL TO CRESCENT LAKE
- MARIPOSA GROVE OF BIG TREES 6800 FT
- GROTTO
- STELLA LAKE
- FOREST DRIVE
- MEADOW DRIVE
- WAWONA HOTEL
- STORE
- LAKE 4046
- INDIAN CAMP
- MEADOW
- BROOK
- LIGHTNING TRAIL
- MEADOW DRIVE
- TRAIL TO BIG TREES
- FOUR MILE
- RIVER VIEW
- BIG TREE ROAD
- U.S.M. CAMP
- WAWONA POINT
- MARIPOSA BIG TREES
- GUARDIAN
- CABIN
- GRIZZLY GIANT
- CALIFORNIA
- FAITHFUL COUPLE
- THE GRACES
- FALLEN MONARCH
- TELESCOPE
- DIAMOND
- POET'S
- GALEN CLARK
- QUEEN
- A.E. WOOD
- U.S.M. CAMP
- FISH HATCHERY
- BIG CREEK
- RUSH CREEK
- ARBORETUM
- TO YOSEMITE 26 MILES
- TO MARIPOSA
- SIGNAL PEAK 7000
- ROAD TO SIGNAL PEAK
- SHAKE CAMP
- ALDER CREEK
- ADLER CREEK
- MEADOW
- ELEVEN MILE MEADOW

Point	Distance Automobile	Point	Distance Coach
Yosemite Valley	26 miles		

Point	Distance Coach	Distance Conv.
Signal Peak		
Wawona Springs		
Fish Hatchery		
Arboretum		
Stella Lake		
Indian Bridge		

Point	Distance Conv. Trail	Distance Conv. Coach
Indian Camp		
Swimming Pool		
Tennis Court		

Point	Distance
Forest Drive	
Meadow Drive	
Alder Creek Falls	
Mt Raymond	

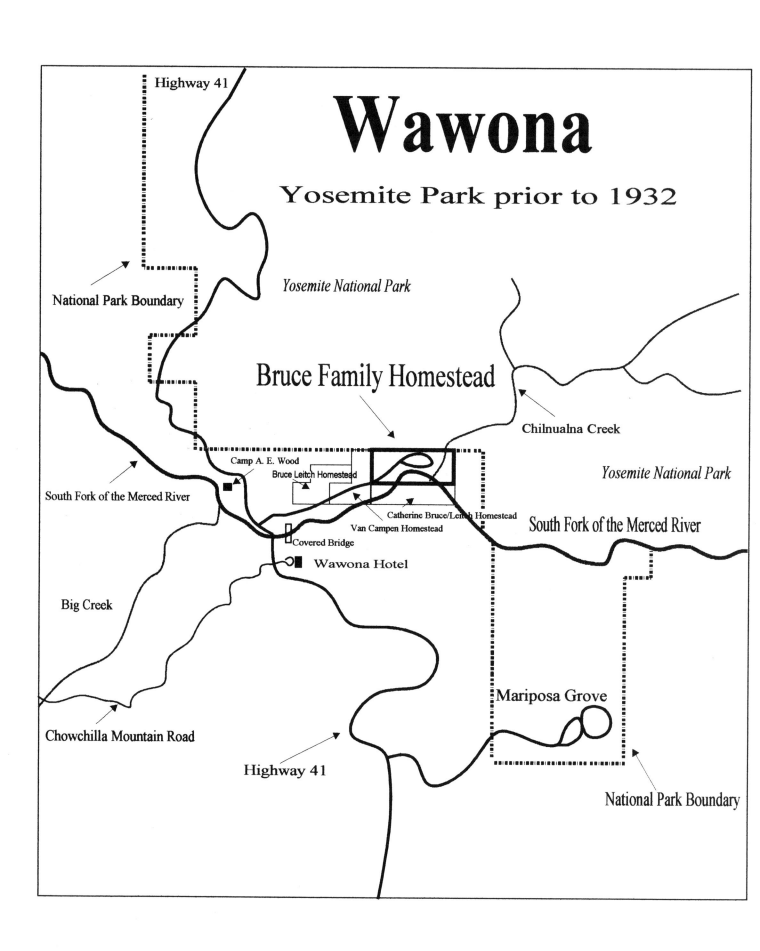

Wawona

Yosemite Park prior to 1932

Highway 41

National Park Boundary

Yosemite National Park

Bruce Family Homestead

Chilnualna Creek

Yosemite National Park

Camp A. E. Wood

Bruce Leitch Homestead

Catherine Bruce/Leitch Homestead

Van Campen Homestead

South Fork of the Merced River

South Fork of the Merced River

Covered Bridge

Wawona Hotel

Big Creek

Chowchilla Mountain Road

Mariposa Grove

Highway 41

National Park Boundary

Yosemite's Forgotten Pioneers

The Bruces of Wawona

Annie Reynolds
&
Thomas Bruce Phillips

Published by
Chilnualna Books
P.O. Box 340
El Portal, CA 95318
(209) 379-2215
tbp@yosemite.net

Dedicated to the memory of
Albert and Azelia Bruce
and their descendants,
all of who make this story a history.

Annie Reynolds and Thomas Bruce Phillips
All Rights Reserved. Printed in the United States
Copyright © 1999

ISBN 0-9668150-0-9

Cover design by Larry Van Dyke
Cover sketch of Homestead House
by B Weiss

Contents

Preface   viii

Acknowledgments   ix

Introduction   x

Foreword   xi

Chapter 1 The Early Adventurers   1

Chapter 2 West to the Sierra   9

Chapter 3 Fire!   18

Chapter 4 The Scandal   21

Chapter 5 The Love Letters   24

Chapter 6 The Wedding   28

Chapter 7 Letters From a Distant Land   38

Chapter 8 Big Tree Station: The Together Times   45

Chapter 9 The Homestead   52

Chapter 10 School Days   62

Chapter 11 Sons of Chilnualna   65

Chapter 12 Daughters of Chilnualna   74

Chapter 13 Winding Down   78

Chapter 14 The Man Who Went to War   84

Chapter 15 The Cougar Hunter   90

Chapter 16 Camp Chilnualna   93

Chapter 17 The Return   95

Chapter 18 Recollections   99

Epilogue   106

Appendix   109

Bibliography   111

Index   113

Preface

It has been written that Robert Bruce (1554–1631) was blessed with a special gift. In his time he was the leading churchman in Edinburgh, Scotland. In 1671, his biographer, Robert Fleming, wrote of Bruce's supernatural experiences, but omitted much because "they would seem so strange and marvelous." Robert Bruce had a prophetic and a healing ministry and his healing of those afflicted with serious maladies is well-authenticated. Fleming did mention many of Robert Bruce's encounters. There were angelic visitations, the voice of God, physical manifestations of the Holy Spirit in meetings and bright lights appearing in the darkness. What he refrained from writing is difficult to imagine.

The ancestral home, "House on the Green" came to Charles Bruce through his marriage to Jean Lindsay. Known also as "Castle on the Green," it was located on the banks of the Tay River in Scotland and built by the Mercer family in 1788.

Originally, this site saw the "Temple of Mars," which was built by the invading Romans, and before them a structure erected by the ancient Picts.

Acknowledgments

Sometimes it takes a village to write a book.

One of the most important elements of recognition here is to give thanks to all the Bruce descendants who saved the family letters, pictures and records through the years. Without them so much of history would be lost and this book would not have come into being. Those members are Roberta Bruce Phillips, Maddalena (Skookie) Gartin, Cecilia Johnsen Laxton, Catherine Stephan Hartske, Gloria Hope Higbee, William Morris Bruce, Barton Douglas Bruce, Nellie Spelt Graham, William (Wally) Bruce II, William Wallace Bruce III, Charlotte Gibner Train, Margaret Bruce, and Linda Bruce.

Linda Eade of the Yosemite Research Library was a special help, as was Dorothy O'Brien of the California Genealogical Society and Muriel Powers of the Mariposa Research Library.

Other sources who offered information were Albert Gordon, Shirley Sargent, Norman and Pat May, Leroy Radanovich, Malcom and Anita Fulmer and Pat Wildt.

Jane Bentle edited the manuscript for her sister. Her generously-given help and expertise elicit something beyond appreciation.

Francis and Nell Donohoe shared their memories from a time they, too, spent in Yosemite. Nell is descended from pioneers John and Bridget Degan.

Ernest Matschke made available Cavalry material, from which the Wawona Cavalry days' episodes were drawn.

Peter Browning, publisher of Great West Books and author of *Yosemite Place Names*, designed the interior of the book. Larry Van Dyke of Wilderness Press designed the cover.

The pen and ink drawing of the homestead house was done by that wonderful artist, B Weiss.

And to my son, John Reynolds, I offer special thanks for his insights, which often presented another angle of thought. He kept the faith.

Without any one of the above, some little part of this book would surely be missing.

Annie Reynolds
September 3, 1999

Introduction

Within Yosemite National Park, at Wawona, there has been created a Living History Center, complete with early buildings of a past Yosemite-time. Volunteers steeped in the history of these past times, as represented by the old buildings, address visitors with greetings and a rundown of that special time. They know no future time.

Cara Morrison, who runs a school on Whitlock road, took her eager students on a field trip to this yesterday-land, and they, too, became re-enactors.

Anthony Phillips became Frederick Law Olmstead, Michelle Phillips, nine, and a year younger than Anthony, became Jean Bruce Washburn. Their father, Thomas Bruce Phillips, suddenly found himself cast in the role of Albert Olcott Bruce.

But who was Albert Olcott Bruce? Who was this Jean Bruce Washburn? What part did these people play in Yosemite's development? The children asked their father everything they could think to ask, and he had to admit he did not know all that much about his ancestors. But he certainly found out.

He began a meticulous research which took him on a fascinating journey outside Mariposa, California, to Perth, Scotland, Williamsburg, New York, New Orleans and Cuba; and he tracked them all— the early Bruces who had ventured so far from home and embarked on their own varied adventures.

Members of his family, he found, had a treasury of letters dating back to 1808. Today became as exciting as yesterday had been as he tracked his forebears. The result of this ongoing search has yielded about eight tightly stuffed volumes of the lives of people Tom heretofore had never thought much about. And the search became so exciting he couldn't stop.

Now, he could tell his children anything they wanted to know about the family heritage.

Foreword

"You know we are a fortunate clan," William Wallace (Wally) Bruce II remarked with pride in 1980 at a Bruce family reunion. "We are a fortunate family in that our early beginnings were two exceptional people."

He was referring to Albert Olcott Bruce and Albert's wife, Azelia Van Campen Bruce, and he was certainly correct in his heartfelt evaluation of his grandparents. They were among Yosemite's earliest pioneers when they homesteaded in Wawona, spending a lifetime there.

More good fortune yet is in being descended from a family who can be tracked across the Atlantic from a Scotland of the early 1800s, and good fortune in that so many family members became the keepers of countless letters and photos which helped compile the long Bruce saga.

This assortment of inter-family records speaks of innovation, inventiveness and industriousness. It hints of heartbreak, travels with history and tells of both fortune and misfortune. Lastly and wonderfully, it sets down an enduring love story.

Undoubtedly, William Wallace was remembering them all, from those he had heard of to those he knew so well.

THE HEADSTONE

On Sunday, September 8, 1996, a congregation of Bruce descendants met at the Odd Fellows Cemetery in Mariposa, California. They met at the grave of an ancestor, Albert Olcott Bruce, to pay tribute to him and his wife, Azelia, and to honor them with the acknowledgment of the couple's remarkable journey.

Albert had died in 1911, Azelia in 1918. No one could say exactly why it had taken 78 years to mark the gravesite, or if possibly an old memorial stone had been vandalized, as sometimes happens in this cemetery.

The stone had been set only the previous evening and only after Thomas Bruce Phillips, the prime inspiration and instigator of the occasion, had suffered heart palpitations, anxieties and a serious dread that the setting of the stone might not be finished by the proposed meeting time. The man who had been contracted to do the work failed to show up.

Tom's wife, Juanita, flew into action. First soaking the spot with a sprinkler to soften the hard-packed earth into a more pliable condition, she then hurried down Highway 140 to Merced to buy cement and boards for molding. It was Saturday afternoon and the necessary Mariposa stores were closed.

She and the children dug. One of the kids hit a rock. "What's that?" he wondered, perhaps fearing he was close to unearthing a body beneath his spade. With the forms fixed in place and the cement poured, Tom set the headstone. No one doubted that Azelia and Albert would have been proud.

It all began with that field trip to Wawona, which in turn instigated the long search into family history. Tom, great-grandson to the couple, and his mother, Roberta Bruce Spelt Phillips, granddaughter, compiled and published a book, *The Bruce Family—History in Letters*, which they then sold to any interested family member. The proceeds went toward the purchase of the memorial headstone for Albert and Azelia. What finer tribute?

1 The Early Adventurers

In early February of the year 1808, Charles Bruce was in Greenock, Scotland, awaiting passage on a ship which would take him to a new world and begin a great odyssey whose scope he could not have imagined. He had traveled from Perth, located in a mountainous region on the Tay River about 32 miles northeast of Edinburgh. There he owned a bakery and was Deacon of the Baker Incorporation, which was most likely comparable to a union president of today. Two of his sons, Charles and Drummond, had paved the way to New York a few years earlier.

Charles' first wife, Jean Lindsay, with whom he had nine children, had died in 1796. The extensive property of Jean's family was to be held for the couple's children, an understanding not quite carried out, later documents reveal, and an understandable bitterness was generated by those children who felt their heritage abused.

It was with his second wife, Jennet, 19 years his junior and often called "The Duchess," whom he wed on December 5, 1797, that Charles left his home and holdings, Castle on the Green, and began the long expedition across the water. Accompanying the couple were his youngest sons, William and John by first wife, Jean, and the children, Margaret and Robert H., by Jennet

Greenock is a seaport on the Firth of Clyde. While here, waiting out the high winds to lessen for a favorable sailing, fifteen-year-old John Bruce began a remarkable history of letters when he wrote his uncle.

Little could he then realize that the coming sea voyage was only the first segment of a much longer voyage and the wild weather a preamble to other storms he would withstand in a long life.

Greenock Feb. 5, 1808

Dear Uncle:

I duly received yours on Saturday from Mr. Craig and was glad to hear from you. I am here in hopes to sail in a few days. We have got our things on board and we have laid in a little sugar and tea for ourselves as the Captain said we could not well want. I have but got a few Silver out of my To (two) pounds but we got it a little down of it upon our sleeping together. Everything is remarkable Dear here on account of so much shipping. The heels of my boots being wore out on the travel which I have got mended. I am about to get a little money from Mr. Craig to pay my lodging as I expect I shall be wanting to have a little sum when I get to New York. If things do not go so well with me as I expect the weather here is extremely bad. Never an hour of above dry weather. Perpetual gales of wind.

Robert sends compliments to you and friends. My compliments to Mr. & Mrs. Archer and family may his kindness to me as well as your own, I will never forget.

Love,
John Bruce

Long letters, detailing their lives with both joys and hardships, synonymous with their great adventures and history, connected the Bruces for years to come.

The times were troubled. Belligerence between Great Britain and France reached out an ugly tentacle to gravely affect the shipping interests of neutral countries, including the United States. Napoleon I, Emperor of France, in 1805, declared a blockade around the British Isles, and that country, to retaliate for this strangulation, created a few naval laws of its own. Ships bound for any French port or any port of French allies should first stop by a British port to pay duty on their cargo. Untenable as this law appeared, the British insisted that any ship which refused was subject to confiscation.

Relations between Great Britain and the United States were strained and growing worse. Great Britain used the practice of impressment, unacceptable to the United States, and too often stopped American ships to impress any on board they perceived as British deserters. In 1807, the British frigate *Leopard* fired on the American frigate *Chesapeake*, thus shortening even more the fuse which was about to be lit to fan the War of 1812.

But fortune was smiling on Charles Bruce. He avoided the worst heat of the coming conflict. It was on March 16, 1808, that he sailed into New York harbor. His credentials were the best. In his adopted city, he continued the family bakery business, his children also leaning the trade. Aware that wealth lay in real estate, he began acquiring land until his holdings totaled 1874 acres, all in the state of New York.

If his native Perth was not to be Charles's city of destiny, New York City surely would be, for on the 25th day of May 1810, alien Charles petitioned the Justice Court of New York for citizenship, and on August 13, 1813, that privilege was granted him. He was fifty-two-years old.

Charles's brother, William, testified on oath and to the satisfaction of the court that: "Charles Bruce has resided six years at least within the State of New York and that during the term aforesaid he has behaved as a man of good moral character attached to the principles of the Constitution of the United States and well disposed to the good order and happiness of the same." As Charles terminated his allegiance to George III, of the United Kingdom of Great Britain and Ireland, he became a true Son of America.

The war between the United States and Great Britain was then one year in the fighting, with an immediate end not in sight as the hostile Great Britain tightened its blockade along the Atlantic Seaboard. The following year, that country's conflict with Napoleon ended, which unfortunately allowed her more manpower to use against the United States.

Charles continued his business, presumably unfettered by the war. In time he sold his Saratoga, New York property to Patrick and Amelia Thomson of New Orleans, holding the note for the balance of the purchase price. He then turned over the note to his son, Drummond, who acquired title to the entire property in 1832 after lengthy negotiations.

Perhaps because of deteriorating health which prevented him keeping pace with earlier aspirations, perhaps feeling he must look after his large holdings in his homeland, Charles returned to Scotland, along with Jennet and their children, Margaret and Robert. Although the considerable estate of his first wife was meant to go to their children upon Charles' death, Charles signed over control of it to Jennet to benefit her until her own death. She lived to an advanced age into the 1840s, and the rightful heirs never received their entitlement.

The seas were to entice more than one Bruce. Charles Jr. involved himself in shipping and became master of a ship sailing between Madagascar and Calcutta. In 1809, a cyclone sank his ship and Charles perished. Only an eight-year-old boy and a doctor, washed ashore on Madagascar, survived the tragedy.

Then on January 9, 1819, the elder Charles was buried in Scotland, it is believed on the family estate. His inheritors continued the expansion of their heritage by investing in real estate, shipping, business ventures and mechanical inventions. They were on their prosperous ways

Drummond, ably equipped with his father, Charles's vision and business acumen, wished to add to his holdings. With this in mind, he traveled to Jamaica and then on to New Orleans, where he bought additional pieces of property with the perceptive intent of subdividing.

New Orleans was a city of courtyards and churches, of culture and commerce. Founded about 1718, it became a U. S. city in 1803 as part of the Louisiana Purchase. Situated as it was on the Gulf of Mexico and only a hundred miles from the mouth of the Mississippi, it was a port city, enjoying great and growing prosperity. With the War of 1812 finally done with, even more decisively so with Andrew Jackson's naval victory at nearby Chalmette, there was now no fear of further British intervention, and trade increased.

Though a 1788 fire had destroyed most of the French Quarter, the area was quickly rebuilt. Standing on Chartres Street was the St. Louis Cathedral and the Cabildo, the latter serving as a place of government—first, the French, and then the Spanish and Americans. The French Market offered produce and food, and on St. Peter Street the Opera House and theatre provided entertainment. It was a propitious time for Drummond to enter this diverse city with his ambitions. As early as 1827 he began investing in property, which included a distillery and cotton fields complete with a work force. He purchased four lots on Louisa Street, a lot on Levee Street, and three lots on Desire Street.

Taking advantage of the times, in 1828 he bought Sally, a seventeen-year-old black girl; and on September 6 of the following year, he traded thirty-five-year-old Ben for a black girl of twenty. Little more of Drummond's personal life can be tracked. Tragically, he, too, died at sea only a few years after his arrival in New Orleans. Facts as to his wealth and intentions can be gathered from his will, drawn up on October 27, 1832. With one noteworthy exception, he left his property, which included his slaves, Ned, Arch, Sally and her daughter, Lucy, to his brothers, William and John Bruce.

To his slave, Paul, Drummond gave his freedom.

A watch given him by "Mammy Mills" was found in Drummond's personal effects, and William suggested it be given to Mrs. Mackie, daughter of the late "Mammy Mills," as a remembrance of both him and the lady.

Although large holdings came to the elder Charles Bruce family through his wealthy first wife, Jean Lindsay, and were expected to go to the children of the couple, the two younger children did not receive their share, and over this deliberate manipulation by second wife, Jennet, a bitterness often surfaced. In his will, Drummond even made mention that he left nothing to the children of Jennet, she not being his mother.

In a letter written to his sister-in-law after his brother Drummond's death, William revealed insights of himself. His affection for her and his disenchantment with his father's will and the final disposition of his mother's property were equally apparent. William's view on slavery, morally at odds with that of Drummond, was made abundantly clear.

From Edinburgh on November 21, 1836, he wrote to her in Jersey City, New Jersey. In part:

My Dear Sister

I have two letters from John, the one stating the Death of our brother, Drummond, and the other intimating his request I would either meet him in New Orleans in two months after the date of his voyage the 5th of Oct., last or that I would forward him a power of Attorney for him to act for me in that City relative to his affairs. Since the date of John's, I have received a letter from a Mr. Issac Preston in closing to me a certified Copy of Drummond's will by which I find he has left considerable property. Now as John and I ever had the fullest

confidence to place in each other, I have forwarded by the ship, *Columbus,* which sailed from Liverpool for New York on the 16th Inst. and the Captain was to see it safely put in the Post Office there, to the care of M. W. Hoffman Esq. of New Orleans. . . .

He also requested the freedom of Drummond's slaves, should such add to their happiness, and in the event such freedom cannot be given, he begged that brother John at least see that they acquire good masters.

Brother Robert had previously written William that his mother had not received any proceeds from the Perth houses for two years and wished William to look into this grievous matter. But William was somewhat disinclined to do so, doubtlessly smarting from his own loss of the inheritance. "I need not trouble myself in the cause as John's interest and mine can only begin when she goes hence."

In his long letter to his esteemed sister-in-law, William mentioned an interesting fact which pointed to his brother's inventive qualities. John would send, he wrote her, a machine of his own invention to London. This was a machine invented in 1832 by John and his son, Charles, that produced a biscuit known as Ship's Biscuit or Hard Tack. John sold this machine all over the Atlantic Seaboard and Europe, as well as four patents to William in Edinburgh.

John J. Bruce, the brother of whom William had just written, was in New Orleans taking care of Drummond's estate when he wrote a letter dated January 5, 1837, to his son, Charles. He was not a happy man. "This is the most trying climate for people of weak constitutions can be. I have been more affected by the sudden and severe changes here than anywhere else." Even as he commented on the disagreeable weather, he admitted to good health, but had one further observation on the subject "a cold kind that penetrates through one and great coats are even of more use here than at the north."

John apparently had thought that the weather that far South would be of a gentler nature and had given both his great coat and a light coat to Drummond's slave, Ned. One day on the levee he met Ned rolling cotton, and Ned was wearing John's benevolent gift of the great coat, and the giver lamented his premature act of giving up his coat in such chilling weather. The benefactor of the coat replied that he thought he would miss it. "I knowed so when you give it me, but it come berry good to me."

Sensibly, Ned kept the coat which helped protect him against the cold atop that levee.

The disposition of Drummond's considerable property would likely take John until spring, John wrote his son. He feared that William might wish to rush the sale to obtain his share. Such action would surely be a sacrifice in the expanding city of New Orleans, he went on to say. He was desirous of obtaining all the Distillery Lots for himself, feeling certain all the properties would rise in value. However, he refuted this idea in the same paragraph when he told Charles that he wished he was rid of the interest he had there. The wet chill was taking its toll on him.

Perhaps because it was January and New Orleans was frightfully cold, perhaps because he had the whole of the affairs in his hands, John was a trifle petulant in his letter, advising Charles not to come to this place, nor had he any intent to himself return. He was hard put to find any charm in the city. If only he had not given away his great coat.

Before John signed himself off as an affectionate father, he laid forth a lesson for his son's reply "write close like this and don't omit to commence persons' names with Capitals and sentences likewise. I leave you to get what you can for Patent Rights. I give up all claim to profit from it to you three. I want to prove to you that I never wished to live for myself alone, that the happiness of my family is mine."

And then he became further a parent with an admonishing P. S. aimed at better correspondence: "Your first express was folded so I had to tear it in pieces to get it open, here is a pattern to you for the future to fold letter by."

At this time, John belonged to the American Institute of Inventors in New York City. He possessed the great gift of creativity in machinery. And he was also a vocal man who, when he perceived the need, was unafraid to speak for truth and justice. While still in the East, he and John Greenleaf Whittier petitioned Congress to stop the brutal thrashing in the Navy, which left bloodied backs. He also became impassioned before Congress concerning the imprisonment of debtors. This plea came from his own regrettable experience when, having lost his receipt for a payment, he was thrown into debtors' prison.

On the 13th day of March in the year 1832, John and Charles Bruce were in custody of a document attesting to their invention of a machine which manufactured Ship Biscuits, Pilot Bread, Crackers and the like, which were foods important for ships to carry on long voyages. The document was a legal paper with the Seal of the United States affixed. It bore the name of Edward Livingston, Secretary of State, and the name of Andrew Jackson, President of the United States. This important paper affirmed by the government of their country did not end their troubles, however.

When Drummond passed away, John and William inherited his vast land holdings. With the help of their attorney, James Humphrey, they struck a deal in which William would get most of Drummond's land in exchange for the four machine patents in Britain, which John had previously sold to William.

The attorney was supposed to act as a holding company for the property and the patent rights to the Biscuit-making machine, but somewhere along the course of this legal action, Humphrey ended up with the land in his name. Whether it was by the lawyer's clever design and legal maneuvering was not corroborated, but his actions were suspect. John sued Humphrey (and therefore William) to get the agreement completed, the deal stating that "part of the land would be sold to pay the expenses of Property Taxes, Patent Costs and Attorney's fees."

For years, John and William were involved in vexatious lawsuits over both property and patent rights. Details of the final outcome are unclear, though it seems that patents could not be found and the land was lost to taxes. When John inquired of Humphrey as to what happened, the lawyer claimed he attempted time and again to get more instructions from William, but was never able to contact him. Humphrey then felt he was discharged from paying taxes on property that the owner failed to show interest in, adding that the last time he saw the Patents they were with William Bruce as he left for Scotland sometime after 1841. John attempted having the property turned back over to him since he was the last legal owner, but by then the cost in taxes was too great. The patents and the land were valued at well over one million dollars.

The two men's fight for their rightful property, both real estate and patented Biscuit making machine, took an incredibly long time, from 1836 to 1861, and left them with only what must have been stress coupled with frustration.

Nine children filled the John J. and Elizabeth Rice Bruce household of Williamsburgh,[1] New York, beginning with the birth of William in 1815. Following were Charles, John Jr., Elizabeth, Robert Kale, Catherine, Jean, Fannie and Albert. As well as from geographic locations, professions and character assessments can be gleaned from family letters. Catherine married Bruce Leitch, a local Justice of the Peace, and Robert Kale and John Jr. ventured to Cuba.

In a letter of January 18, 1854, sixteen-year-old Jean wrote to John, then in Cuba, and her words were revelatory:

Dear John,

Your good kind comforting letter to Mother has been received and it really revived and cheered her much to hear of your keeping in such excellent health and spirits. Your generous present came to hand some time ago and a portion has already been spent out of your residence there. I hope some permanent fortune may arise and enable you to fulfill your affectionate and noble intentions for you deserve if ever man did, the best of success and happiness, and all at home desire it for you so earnestly that it will not fail to bless you. All thank you for your generous gift to Mother as they well may, as it will minister to all and give a more cheerful and independent feeling instead of that gloom or apprehension. Mother is again better in health than for the year before. The Doctor who attended her was very skillful and relieved her more rapidly and surely than any who was ever called to her. She is happier and more contented than for some time past. Your letters have been a consolation to her they

always speak so mildly and kindly that they bring a healing and reviving influence that our hearts feel but words may not express. They are so full of tenderness so different from any letters we ever received before.

Father's business is going on, though I cannot say to much advantage, but with prospects of improving. He has numerous orders to fill, but no new partner yet, though Mr. Moore and him parted company some weeks ago.

Albert is anxious to go to Cuba, but the employers have made no decision though Father has called upon them several times. (The General Phelps) said they would send him and so it rests at present.

Jean wrote further of the trunk being sent to Nueritas, Cuba, on the ship, *William H. Spear,* and which would be directed to the U. S. Consul. She went on:

There is in the trunk six shirts, four Linen bosomed and two to wear about your work, also four neck ties, five pocket handkerchiefs, one pair common pants, six pairs socks accompanied by a pair of blankets and a Hammock. We could not get a cot Hammock, and so Father bought this ... Do not trouble yourself about sending fruit for I understand from your last account you are not living in the heart of orchards as I before imagined. For I dreamed that Island made up of fruit, flowers and sunshine. A second Eden with a lot of monsters destroying its beauties and poisoning its atmosphere. Do be careful of all letters or papers and destroy any that might give offense, as you have no interest political or otherwise in the affairs of that Country and unmeant trifles often lead to great troubles.

For one so young, Jean possessed a keen insight into government and diplomacy. And then she shared with her brother a most unusual happening before relating other family matters.

Fanny and I just for sport last night, laid our hands upon one of our light bedroom tables.

---

1 Williamsburgh was at that time a town located in King County, New York on the western end of Long Island on the East River. It was incorporated with Brooklyn in 1855, and is today part of the city of New York.

It soon became magnetized and shivered and danced Nervously. All the time, Fanny's figure trembled with electricity while I remained firm. Seemingly acting on her, while the table quivered, I asked if any spirits were present. It rapped loudly. I inquired for you. It said you were well and would yet be well off. It said I was a Medium. That Fanny was not.

It told the fortunes of all the family. Said you would yet get married. That Fanny and I would do the same in the course of two years. That Charles and Bill had suffered much in California, that they were thinner than when we saw them last, and that they would not get rich in those regions. It also said Father and Mother should be happy in their age. that all our family would be happier then heretofore. That the world respected us more for the concerts we gave, that Fanny and I would leave fame after us, that mine would be greatest, and really told us most charming news, told us Auld was indifferent to our fates and Leitch was an Enemy. That Kate would be widowed in four years and marry again. So take it for what it's worth. I wish some of the good prophecies would come true. Don't imagine us crazy it is all fun.

Apparently, Jean was not concerned by the unusualness of this visitation, but accepted the intervention with an amount of practicality. In time, brother Robert Kale would become distraught by a similar invasion by the spirit world into his soul.

Not only was Albert desirous of passage to Cuba, but someone by the name of Jack had already saved thirty dollars toward his own intent to go there. Jean went on to apprise John of her opinion that such a journey for Albert would be more advantageous to him than going to California where the family that had migrated there had "not yet received the fulfillment of their prospects."

Inspired with the romantic, Jean went on to express her wishes:

I hope you'll look out for a dark eyed Senorita, whose heart may bring with it a little golden treasure to make home a comfortable place, as the raps say, you are certainly to be married. May you get a gentle affectionate darling unlike Bob's Tigress, to whom he has dutifully returned.

She was referring to Robert Kale who was tortured not only by the spirits, but a spirited wife, Jane, whose actions helped him flee to Cuba.

Her long letter's ending paragraph gave an interesting insight to her own interests and accomplishments.

We won't publish in the Dispatch anymore as they have acted insolent to us of late. I got twelve dollars for my address from Jack. He made over sixty. We've not been paid for the Wall Street Journal one yet, tho' the time has gone by so long, it's like all other art from that quarter. Leitch is out of office and has hopes of a situation in the patent department. . . .

I am Your affectionate Sister, Jean

Jean was already becoming a poet of some repute. Her reference of payment for "an address" was likely for some writing she had done for either a magazine or newspaper.

Writing to John, she adamantly voiced a desire for liberation, a spirited attitude that would manifest itself through her coming years. She indicated a wish that brother Bill, who had emigrated to Cali-

Albert Olcott Bruce, both a mechanic and a miner, fulfilled his destiny in a place akin to Paradise— Wawona. Portrait by I. W. Taber Studio in San Francisco. His suit was navy blue.
(Roberta Bruce Phillips Collection.)

fornia would fulfill his intent to send the girls "something in the Spring. It will be well if he could do so and we might try our fortunes again. How happy we could be if each had an income and could all be together once more."

It is unclear if Bill helped the hopeful girls on their journey to coveted independence or inherent spirits helped forge the future, but Jean was, in a few years, to know prosperity and enjoy a social position beyond her youthful aspirations.

Albert Olcott never got to Cuba. Born in New York on March 5, 1837, he was the last son of John J. and Elizabeth Bruce. He worked for General Phelps in Williamsburgh, where his family still lived. He saved his money with the firm intent of joining brother, Robert Kale, on that southerly island of insurgents and revolutions. But instead of embarking on a ship to Cuba, he set sail in 1855 for a different and distant land, California, and joined

Albert Bruce's abiding dream was to own a stamp mill. He began constructing stamp mills with his older brother, Charles, when he first ventured to California in 1855. Pictured here is a five-stamp mill located at the Mariposa County History Center. There is little doubt of its working capabilities when its roaring clank reverberates over half the county. *(Mariposa County History Center.)*

his brothers in Mariposa County. He was then eighteen years old.

He began his career there by working with William and Charles in their established machine shop, and although he had arrived in the area with engineering expertise, he began learning other trades that would help invent the rest of his life. He learned blacksmithing, gunsmithing and everything possible about machinery. With this varied background, he began an independent career as a mining engineer when he went to work for the Washington Mine near Hornitos, California.

When the gold rush began, miners searched for "placer gold," gold on the surface of the land. The "placer gold" soon played out and a need to search for the source of the gold came about. It was found that within the white rock veins of quartz lay the true Mother Lode. At first, Spanish arrastras were used to free the gold from the quartz. An arrastra was a simple device consisting of a rock-lined pit in which pieces of quartz would be placed while another larger rock was used to crush the quartz into dust. The large rock was pulled around the arrastra by a mule, horse, or miner. The quartz dust would then be washed away leaving the gold. This method proved too slow and time-consuming so a more mechanical device would replace the arrastra.

The stamp mill worked to the same end that the arrastra did but with much more efficiency and noise. When the ore was brought out of the mine it would be broken into fist-size pieces by sledgehammers and fed in the mill. The stamp mill was usually a two-story structure in which the gold-bearing ore would be processed. The ore would enter the uppermost floor where the larger pieces would be separated and the smaller pieces would fall into the stamps. The larger pieces would be ground into smaller pieces by metal crushing plates before entering the stamp itself. The stamp consisted of heavy metal plates attached to rods that would be lifted up mechanically and dropped on the quartz, crushing it into a powder. The metal plates or hammers weighed approximately 1,750 pounds.

The crushed ore was then washed out onto large sluice-like copper plates coated with mercury. The mercury formed an amalgam with the gold dust. The mixture was then boiled till the mercury boiled off leaving the gold dust. Later cyanide would also be used to remove more waste material from the gold.

Stamp mills were built in many different forms from one stamp to one hundred stamps depending on the financing and anticipated return. They were powered by water or electricity.

In 1867, the first 10-stamp mill in the area was erected near the Washington Mine by Albert and Mose Rodgers, the mine's owner, who was a recently liberated slave. Albert worked at this mine until March of 1874 when he took a position with the Belmont Silver Mining Company in Nevada. But before he went to Belmont, far more important aspects of his life would transpire.

By the time this portrait was taken, probably about 1870, John J. Bruce had done it all. From his native Scotland to his adopted Sierra, he had thrived on the love of his children and his faith in God.
(Roberta Bruce Phillips Collection.)

John Jay Cook was a man whose considerable ambition and perception carried him through his long life. Born on June 4, 1837, in Dutchess County, New York State, he abandoned farm life young when he ran away from the farm to work at a dry goods store on Grand Street in the Eastern District of New York City. His mettle was proved within a few years when he became a partner in that business. Gone forever was the farm boy. His ambitions were on the ascendancy, on a parallel course with his expertise. He soon became a member of the silk and lace import house of Bowen, MacNamee & Co. of Broadway, New York City.

His interests took diversified courses, leading him to co-found the first Young Women's Seminary in the United States. He also became a pharmacist; a trade possibly learned from Dr. Steven Cook, his brother. In that era pharmacy was studied under a doctor. He was also a Republican of an uncompromising nature.

It is probable that John Jay Cook and John J. Bruce met through one of their ongoing business enterprises in the same area, and therefore put into motion part of Jean's prophecy that she shared with brother, John, in her 1854 letter. Fanny, youngest daughter of John J., was soon to marry.

Fanny's romance with John Jay Cook was not free of all obstacles leading to unfettered joy, however. Her mother had been suffering a grave illness for over four years, and now that lady who had borne her trials with such stoicism knew her time of departing was near. It was her wish that Fanny and her suitor marry at her bedside.

This the couple did in a ceremony performed by Reverend W. Partridge on Sunday, October 31, 1858. Only eight days later, on Monday, November 8, 1858, Elizabeth passed away.

John Bruce was still embroiled in the litigation over his patent rights and real estate. A deposition taken on January 26, 1861 attested to his various residences since the day he stepped on American shores and also stated an interesting fact. He was going to make a new home in Mariposa, California. He was on the threshold of shaping the fortune and destiny of the Bruce family.

The years of fighting for his rights, the misunderstandings with the lawyer, James Humphrey, and the perpetual uncertainties attendant to this situation probably caused him a disenchantment with life on the Eastern Seaboard. He had lost his wife, and three of his sons were already in California. He was sixty-nine years old and ready to tackle a new beginning.

John Jay Cook also geared up for a new life. He sold his vast holdings for $150,000 and with his in-laws and his wealth headed West. It was his personal Manifest Destiny.

John J. Bruce's daughter, Elizabeth, had married a man surnamed Auld, and they chose to stay behind. Catherine had married Bruce Leitch, a Justice of the Peace in New York, and Jean was single. With his daughters and their husbands, John Jay Cook and Bruce Leitch, John J. began the final segment of his long and often tortuous journey.

2 West to the Sierra

Robert Kale Bruce never went West to California. Instead, he took passage to Cuba, traveling between that country and the United States from the 1850s to the late 1800s. He entered a country as full of unrest as was his own soul.

Cuba was a land of internal turmoil, instigated by several factions, the primary one being Spain, who had long regarded Cuba as hers by way of Columbus touching shore there in 1492. Unrest, revolt and conspiracies ran rampant, tormenting the island and its people. But despite revolutions and uprisings, Robert Kale, a civil engineer and master mechanic, decided to make his fortune in Cuba. Once there, he established a business building machinery.

A letter of 1855 is a declaration of his new company's intent, expertise and ambition:

Puerto Principe, Cuba
The 1st of February, 1855

GENTLEMEN:

We beg leave to make known to you that we have formed this date a partnership, under the firm of Bruce & Co., for the purpose of transacting a General Commission Business.

Sufficient means and ample experience will enable us to execute, to your entire satisfaction, any commissions you may be pleased to place in our hands.

Respectfully soliciting your important patronage, and hoping soon to establish a lively, prosperous and satisfactory intercourse with your highly respectable house, we remain,

Gentlemen,
Your obed't Serv'ts
BRUCE and CO.

Although the letter was sent to potentially interested customers in early 1855, with the partnership including Robert's father, John J., and likely his brother, John Jr., the elder Bruce gave notice only six months later that he was retiring from the new firm.

PARTNERSHIP NOTICE:

Notice is hereby given that John J. Bruce Sr. retired from the late firm of "Bruce And Co." Company merchants, Puerto Principe, Island of Cuba on or about the first of August last under and in. Dated New York 30th Oct. 1855, pursuance of the Laws of the island of Cuba and that his act of retirement has been lodged in the proper notary office at Puerto Principe. New York 30th Oct. 1855.

There is no evidence that the elder Bruce ever resided in Cuba, for in his deposition taken at the time of his legal entanglements, he made no mention of residing there. Neither is it known why he left the firm. Perhaps the call to California was stronger than the call to Cuba.

In the West, Mariposa County, too, was rife with problems; the Nation was awash with problems. And so John J., as had his father, rode the rails of a tumultuous time.

Although gold had been discovered in Georgia in 1829, the general cry in the country was but a murmur compared to that in the West when James Marshall discovered a tiny speck of gold in a tailrace at Coloma on the American River. It was January 24, 1848. A great change began to stir the land. It caused the man for whom Marshall worked, John Sutter, to lose his business when men trampled his forested holdings. It inspired men to desert their ships in port, their homes and often, their families, to rush to the gold fields, and brought into the soon-to-be state of California a new surge of eager immigrants. And the discovery soon gave birth to the Sierra foothill town of Mariposa, to which John Bruce headed.

The subsequent gold years saw California fill up and grow up fast. Single men and married men, men from other countries and now and then a woman, began a steady migration that quickly begot an addendum to the nation. It usurped the residency of both the Native Americans and the Spanish-Mexicans and held the land captive to mines, houses, tents and businesses and even a few roads to reach them.

It was doubtlessly the prospects of prosperity, coupled with that inherent sense of adventure which had propelled the family to America over 40 years earlier, that took John J.'s sons to the frontiers of the West. The opening of the quartz veins had opened up much more -- the promise of opportunity whose scope could only be speculated upon. It was a time to get rich, given luck and fortitude.

Charles Bruce was born in Harlem, New York, in 1816. He married Mary Ann Bridle, a native of Australia, and they had one child, Johnny Bridle, born in 1838. Mary Ann died while the family lived in New Orleans, and in 1850, Charles, his son and his brother William, went to California to the gold-

Charles Bruce—with his brother William and son, Johnny Bridle—went west in 1850 to try his fortune. *(Roberta Bruce Phillips Collection.)*

prospecting area known as Mariposa. In this new town any business established was bound to be a welcome one. The Charles Bruce Co. built a mill on Saxton Creek, about two miles down from the William Van Campen Mill.

In 1862, John Bruce Jr. left Cuba to join his brothers in Mariposa.

Around 1864, Charles was elected Justice of the Peace, and in this capacity saw the history of the area unfold as his duties ranged from the joyous to the judicial side of misdeeds. Marriages and miscreants--he saw them all. With his son and brothers, he held several quartz mining claims all over the county.

At the time of the senior Bruce's arrival, the town already had its roots firmly implanted and flourishing in the ground. By 1849, Colonel Archie Stevenson, a county merchant, had opened a store. A courthouse stood up on the hill, the Challenge Saloon stood at Main and 5th Streets. Proprietors Weber and Schlageter proudly advertised their Weber House, also on Main Street, as having the best board and lodging at reasonable rates, as well as Lager Beer from the Mariposa Brewery. With hotels, saloons, a post office, a Board of Supervisors and a newspaper, the town showed every sign of prosperity. Although the first flush of gold fever was paling, merchants still sold mining supplies.

In that same year, another discovery higher in the Sierra provoked some attention. Some would later claim that a hunter named Hogg first stumbled upon it. More credence was afforded Sheriff Burney of Mariposa County. While chasing Indians who were suspected of stealing some cattle, Sheriff Burney entered a grove of giant sequoias. Touching the gold made a few people rich and its temptation gave hope to thousands. But the grove of extraordinarily large trees, later known as the Mariposa Grove of Big Trees, invested a special awe in the millions who would later enjoy the sight of it.

This was a time of discoveries. After the gold, another discovery began to add commerce to the town and stir the Nation. Farther up into the Sierra, the Merced River ran through a long canyon which ended in a remarkable valley walled with granite spires and domes. It was a place of waterfalls and grassy meadows and thick forests.

On March 27, 1851, the recently mustered Mariposa Battalion was sent to this area to rout the

In 1860 the town of Mariposa was growing rapidly. The gold and attendant ambitions demanded it.
(Leroy Radanovich Collection.)

Indian residents, some of whom were suspected of depredations|against nearby mining camps. In charge of the Battalion was Major James Savage, who had established trading posts on both the Fresno River and the South Fork of the Merced River. He later built Fort Bishop further along the Fresno River, at that time still a part of Mariposa County. With the Company, slogging through snow as deep as four feet in places, was a four-dollar-per-day private, Lafayette Houghton Bunnell, himself recently from the mining camps. This private was endowed with a keen sense of observation and appreciation of what he beheld. From a vantage point later to be aptly known as Old Inspiration Point, he looked down into a wondrous valley and was overcome with an awe that would move him to describe for posterity the sights he viewed that day.

After much consideration, and with the eventual agreement of other members of the company of 57, Bunnell named this place Yo Semite, which means "a large grizzly bear."

Later, the Indian chief, Ten-ei-ya, told him that

he and his two companions, James M. Roan and George H. Crenshaw, were the first white men to enter the Valley. He assured him that it could not have been entered without his knowledge.

In four years, journalist James Hutchings wrote of the Valley's enchantment, artist Thomas Ayres confirmed its beauty with his paintings, and innkeepers had erected rough lodgings for the benefit of eager tourists who sought to share its splendors.

Thus, Mariposa town was to beckon another industry to supplant the eventual dwindling output of the gold mines. Tourism came to town.

It is likely that John J. Bruce sought to steer his four sons into businesses more amenable to growth and prosperity than the mining claims which interested them. It is also probable that in his retirement years, with his genius for the mechanical, he helped in his sons' machine shop.

Misfortune too soon was bestowed upon the family when nature visited in an overabundance. The rains came. Beginning in November of 1861, the storms lasted well into the New Year. Before they ended, the Merced River had swept away many bridges, and the waters of Mariposa Creek, on whose bank the Bruce Brothers Shop was located, swept away all its bridges.

The machine shop went over endways into the rushing torrent. An acre or two of rain-soaked mountain slid to a depth of 40 or 50 feet, and this avalanche roared with the anger of thunder. Fortunately for those residents situated on the western bank of Mariposa Creek, it was accompanied by a great rush of water which carried off the mud into a deep gulch. It was one of the worst times any of the early settlers could recall enduring.

The roads to both Bridgeport and Morman Bar were closed due to high water, and communication with the outside world was as severed as the roads.

Out of 100,000 cattle in San Joaquin County, only 10,000 survived. Twelve Chinamen drowned in Pleasant Valley. Flumes were torn out, orchards washed away, mining equipment lost and in some areas, bars of sand replaced the fertile soil. It was a disaster to rival the town's terrible fire of 1858.

As young as the town was, culture and entertainment abounded for the pleasure of its inhabitants. Despite the continuing heavy rains, the 2nd Annual Mariposa Mud-Sills Ball was held on January 1, 1862, at the Concert Hall. Supper was furnished by J. Weber of the Weber Hotel. Tickets cost $3 and the music was furnished by Myer's Quadrille Band. Considering the inclement weather, the ball saw a large gathering, rivaling that of the Odd Fellows Ball, an event given two years earlier.

Dancing continued until daylight. One set was made merrier by the rendering of two Irish songs by John J. Bruce. John was later described as a man of olden times, and the audience showed appreciation with their hearty applause. The New Year was met with gaiety.

Proceeds from the ball were distributed equitably among the schools. Mariposa Public School was enhanced by $50; to the Guadalupe School, $20; and also $20 to Sherlock School. Johnny Bridle Bruce acted as treasurer of this affair and his father, Charles, was one of nine on the Committee of Introduction.

And the rains continued.

Forty-niner Peter Gordon, another of the town's earliest settlers, made his way to Stockton for news of the world. It was a perilous journey, even for one

so intrepid, and when no word was reported of him, he was feared drowned. Jamestown was swept away. The Merced River rose 60 feet above its low water mark, and at McCabe's Flat, downriver from Yo Semite, a huge section of mountain slid into the river, temporarily damming it. The water rushed over this barrier and wiped away Benton Mills.

Living there since being employed as a chemist and amalgamator for the mine in 1860 was Lewis Fuller Jones and his family, friends of owner John C. Frémont. The river rose steadily, and sensing the ultimate threat of flooding, Lewis Jones decided to move his family to higher ground. This proved to be a sensible decision. As they fled, Sarah Jones grabbed her husband's treasured Guarnerius violin, his flute and her gold watch, and, with the clothing they wore, that was what they escaped with.

Across endless sweeps of water, stretches of mud and overturned earth and desolation, Peter Gordon returned after eight days to Mariposa with news of the flood's ravaging. His had been an extraordinary feat of traversing swollen rivers and flooded fields.

It was a bad time for Mariposa; it was a worse one for the Nation. The Country was immersed in another sort of upheaval, precipitated by the secession from the Union on December 20, 1860, of South Carolina and quickly followed with like action of ten more Southern states. The Secessionist War, or the Civil War, ate into the West and subsequently into the attitudes and opinions of Mariposa's townspeople.

In the long year of 1862 both home and the Nation suffered unrest on a major scale. The *Mariposa Gazette* was punctuated with news, occasionally good, but as often bad, as the war escalated. The news of January 1862 reported that 10,000 Rebels were routed at Somerset, Kentucky. Publisher A. M. Swaney picked up and reprinted the item in his *Gazette*, undoubtedly with satisfied glee.

Closer to home, the Fisher & Co. Stage Line advertised its services. The stage left Stockton on alternate days at six in the morning, passing through Snellingville and Phillip's Ferry and arriving at Hornitos at seven in the evening. The continuing journey began the next morning at three, passed through Bear Valley and reached Mariposa at eleven the same morning. The fare to Mariposa was $10.

Officials kept busy. A bill was presented to the Legislature to prevent Chinamen from holding mining claims. The Chinese people, as well as the Indian people and the Mexican people, had all worked gold claims or were in the employ of miners who held claims. The less the gold showed, the more the white settlers resented the intrusion of other nationalities working the claims for themselves.

Around the same time a Mariposa miner of middle years, suffering from consumption, had been advised to seek a better climate for his last

Galen Clark, one of the early pilgrims to the area, stood before the Haverford Tree.
(*Morrie Bruce Collection.*)

few months of life. With this sentence of death upon him, Galen Clark moved upward in the Sierra to a place the Indian people called Pallahchun, located on the South Fork of the Merced River. There he built a rude cabin. He soon turned his dwelling place into a hostelry for the accommodation of travelers who were on the increase to the area and the valley of Yo Semite, a short distance beyond. The only way from Mariposa to reach this place was on a tortuous Indian trail over 6500-foot Chowchilla Mountain. It was a tough track. A wagon road was desperately needed.

In addition to the Bruces and Cooks, early families daring to find their futures in a new frontier were the Washhurns and the Van Campens. Their lives would soon intersect and interlock.

The Van Campens had begun their own long journey years earlier, when in the 1600s they left Holland to settle on the East Coast. The Dutch loved settling on rivers and inlets and were therefore happy with the New York and New Jersey areas.

Harriet Angeline Howard could trace her lineage to the country's beginning. Both her grandfather and father fought in the Revolution of 1776 and the War of 1812. When she was 25, she married William Van Campen, descendant of Cornelius Van Campen, one of the early settlers of New Jersey.

Ira Van Campen, brother of William, was the first in his family to tackle the westward journey. He began his trek in 1848, crossing the plains in an oxen-pulled covered wagon. Settling in Hornitos, a

Harriet Howard, wife of William Van Campen and mother to Azelia, in an 1837 portrait by Robert Bullard. Harriet was no less a pioneer than her husband. The artist was her first cousin, who served as a general in the Civil War.
(*Roberta Bruce Phillips Collection.*)

good-sized mining camp, he soon bought a spread called the Elkhorn Ranch.

When William later joined Ira, he bought a portion of the Elkhorn Ranch.

Ten years later William's family began their own westward journey to join him, traveling the circuitous route by way of Panama. They left New York on the *S. S. Uncle Sam*[1] on December 18, 1859, at ten o'clock in the morning. They crossed the Isthmus of Panama and there, on the western side, boarded the side-wheeler, *S. S. North Star* for the remainder of the voyage to San Francisco. At half past three on the afternoon of January 10, 1860, Harriet and her three children, Aziel Barnes, Howard and Azelia Villette, sailed through the Golden Gate.[2]

Albert Henry Washburn was, like the Bruces, the Van Campens and John Jay Cook, a transplanted New Englander. His lineage is traced to the Washbournes of Knights' Washbourne, England. About 1630, a Washbourne sailed for the New World and settled in the Royal Colony of Massachusetts at Duxbury. He had left a comfortable home and position to found a dynasty of Washburns on new shores. Some of his descendants would hold government office and figure prominently in the political and social structures of their time. From this line, Albert Henry, more commonly known as Henry, descended.

Henry's father, Seth, married Rebecca Paine and they produced eight sons. With his second wife, Patty Campbell, he had seven sons, born in quick succession in Randolph, Vermont. Henry was the fifth, born on November 17, 1836.

The discovery of gold in the American River and the subsequent surging of settlers into western lands doubtlessly triggered Henry's trans-continental migration in the 1850s. He was a man of great vision.

He soon settled in Bridgeport, a community five miles outside Mariposa, where he opened a store and bar, raised hogs and operated a mine called the "Washington Buckeye Quartz Mine." Working with him was his brother, Seth Caswell, born on October

13, 1832, four years after the death of their father's first son, also called Seth Caswell.

Years down the road, on July 27, 1926, seventy-eight-year-old Aziel Barnes Van Campen, assuredly aware that history should be recorded, directed a lengthy memoir to Dr. Carl P. Russell and Ernest P. Leavitt of the Yosemite Park Service, in which he recalled the first time he laid eyes on Henry Washburn and his brother, Ed, who had joined him. Aziel was twenty-three in 1861 when he rode by Bridgeport and saw the brothers as they tended to some of their varied interests. But Bridgeport was not to keep the brothers.

Of the Van Campens, it was Azelia who would become the prime player on the Bruce family stage. In 1862, when she was thirteen, her family embarked upon another journey which her brother, Aziel Barnes, would remember all his life and record it, too, for the Yosemite National Park Service and posterity.

He wrote:

July 28, 1862   We left Elkhorn Ranch and went to Sebastopol. (Sebastopol was six miles above Mariposa.)

July 29, 1862   We went by the White and Hatche's sawmill and stop at Cold Springs. (Located at the western base of Chowchilla Mountain.)

July 30, 1862   We arrived at Galen Clark's Station.

July 31, 1862   Galen Clark guided the party to the Big Tree Grove. After reaching the Fallen Monarch, Galen reached under the tree and produced a quart bottle of whiskey. He offered Father Van Campen a drink, but Father refused it, not being a drinking man. Galen then took a drink and placed it back into its hiding place where he might treat himself to another on some future occasion. The party rode thru a fallen tree that was burnt hollow. They started out three abreast but ending up side by side at the end.

---

1. The ship was sunk in Charleston Harbor in 1862 to prevent the British blockade runners from aiding the Southerners with food, ammunition, and firearms.

2. Named by John C. Frémont in the spring of 1846.

Galen Clark pointed out trees to which he has given names to like the "Unfaithful Couple."[3] Upon reaching the upper grove we ate a lunch that Galen Clark provided, of Venison and Sardine sandwiches.

August 1, 1862   We crossed the South Fork of the Merced River on two trees. We continued up a long zigzag trail until we finally reached a beautiful meadow, knee high in grass with snow still in the shady spots. The winter of 1861 had heavier snows than ever before known to white men. We arrived at the foot of Bridalveil Fall at sundown.

August 1, 1862   We registered at the Hutchings Hotel as:
Mr. Wm. Rodger Van Campen
Mrs. Harriet Angeline Van Campen
Master Aziel Barnes Van Campen
Miss Azelia Villette Van Campen

Azelia Van Campen at 16, with a Mona Lisa smile for the photographer. *(Bruce Family Collection.)*

That was the year Mariposa suffered the great flood. The Merced River flooded the Valley floor, its water reaching the porch of the Hotel. Visitors were unable to hike up to see either Vernal or Nevada Falls.

In Azelia Van Campen's portraits her eyes show a woman with a direct gaze and her mouth hints of humor. In some of the many intact letters surviving the years, her friends mention her varied abilities, and in Azelia's own letters, her achievements filter through her many words. She was a woman of exceptional talents and strength, perseverance and passion.

From 1862 through 1867, the Van Campens lived on the Elkhorn Ranch near Hornitos. As a young girl, Azelia was taught sewing and the piano by her accomplished mother, while her father, who had started an orchard and a vineyard and fields of wheat, introduced her to the finer points of farming. All would hold her in good stead. Education was a long-continuing part of her life.

Mariposa County was the largest county ever created in this country, encompassing 25,000 square miles and stretching from Tuolumne County to the North and Los Angeles and San Diego Counties to the South. Later legislation divided this huge area into other counties. Mariposa town did all it could to grow up to match the proportions of the original vast acreage. A bathing facility was established on Main Street, with baths offered for as low as 50 cents. The Washburns began their first inroads into transportation with a livery stable which supplied pack horses for the journey over Chowchilla Mountain to Galen Clark's hostelry, Clark's Station.

Located within a few miles of Mariposa were the prosperous mining camps of Sherlock's, Whitlock's, Agua Frio, Bridgeport and Mormon Bar. West of Mariposa the towns of Hornitos, Quartzburg and Indian Gulch were enjoying limited prosperity. Along the streams, brush shacks and tents of miners stood. With the beginning of quartz mining, Princeton, Bear Valley and Mt. Ophir came into being. The countryside was filling up

The Court was the center for correcting the area's disorders. Innkeeper Schlageter was charged with violation of the Sunday Law which stated that

---

3.   The close growing trees were most likely The Faithful Couple.

no liquor could be sold on Sunday. Mr. Schlageter insisted firmly that such was part of his business and therefore both necessary and legal. His argument was apparently valid, for as he put up his fight, three trials were required before an acquittal verdict was reached.

There was no doubt Justice Charles Bruce was kept busy in the dispensation of justice. Peter Gordon, who had founded one of the town's first hotels, was involved in one of his scrapes when he hit a Chinese lady with his whip. He was assisting the

Charles Bruce, 1816–1880. In his later years, this machinist and miner worked for his brother-in-law, John Jay Cook. *(Roberta Bruce Phillips Collection.)*

tax collector and later claimed this lady was trying to tear off his trousers. In court he failed to aid his defense when he raised the same whip to whack the lady's chief witness. He was fined a small, unrecorded amount.

Robberies were rampant, with the Chinese too often the hapless victims. On one occasion, nine of them were held up by six Mexicans, tied hand and foot and their feet pricked with a Bowie knife before they were relieved of their revolvers and $200.

The streams and quartz veins became increasingly reluctant in their yielding of gold, but an occasional happy find transpired. A quartz vein bearing gold was found in Sherlock Creek after a heavy rain, and at Agua Frio, a piece of nearly pure gold weighing 16 ounces was taken. A consistent yield was also noted at the Sweetwater Mine.

Both mining claims and water rights brought out the rigors of temper and hot action.

At Agua Frio, two companies of Chinese fought over a water ditch and the division of that water. The dispute turned nasty when Tin See grievously wounded Ty in a disregard that they were countrymen. Tin See was brought before Justice Bruce who committed him to prison to await the Grand Jury's action.

Fourth of July celebrations always helped to relieve the tensions of the times and in 1862 tensions were tight, particularly with the area filled with both Unionists and Secessionists. Two balls commemorating that grandest of days were held in Snellings, one given by the Union men and the other by the Secessionists at the Stone House. At a Mormon's Bar celebration, A. F. Washburn captivated the assemblage with a reading of the Declaration of Independence. Dancing at these affairs usually continued until dawn.

The Civil War caused the county to fly two flags as sentiments, harshly divided, proclaimed loyalty to the Union and also to the Confederacy. When Andrew Swaney became the publisher of the *Mariposa Gazette* in November of 1862 he voiced his views rather adamantly about the state of the Union. He wished he could crush the power of the Rebellion in the strong belief the Union should be preserved, he printed.

In 1862 Mariposa, when a Patriotic Fund to aid the Union was begun, it can be noted that the ladies subscribed to the noble cause, independent of their affiliated men. In a long list published in the *Gazette* by name and amount, it was noted that Mrs. A. M. Swaney contributed, separately, as did her husband. Mrs. Angevine Reynolds gave, in addition to her husband's generous offering of $25. Also listed was the contribution of C. Bruce and Bro. for $25, as well as $5 from Miss Jean L. Bruce.

The fires that had ignited that Great Rebellion in the East still flamed, and the war was very much in contention yet by July 4, 1863, the Confederate flag was soon to flutter no more over the establishments of those favoring the Southern cause. Gettysburg. The green, rolling Pennsylvania countryside became a killing ground of awful assaults. It began with Confederate soldiers, many barefoot and looking for shoes, and ended with 51,000 troops dead or wounded. It marked the tide turning in favor of the Union.

Despair enveloped the home front. The public schools of Mariposa closed for lack of funds. Fun alternated with folly, but now it was time to stage a few more galas.

With the merry help of the Princeton Brass Band, the town enjoyed another bang-up affair when the Odd Fellows celebrated their 43rd anniversary in the Western World, beginning with a procession from the Odd Fellows Hall up to the Court House. Dinner was later served at the Concert Hall, and then the dancing began. The dancing had to be of particular delight, for of the attendees 105 were women, the largest number ever gathered together in one place in town.

And on another happy note, Justice Bruce married Mr. Ching Toe to Miss Si Toy on March 23, 1862.

Although nearby Mt. Bullion was commonly referred to as Princeton, the practice was growing out of style when that town's postmaster, John Martin, stated that henceforth all mail meant for that place should be addressed to Mt. Bullion. And again, *Gazette* publisher, Andrew Swaney, sneered at the Copperheads and Secessionists by praising the raising of the Union flag over a Princeton/Mt. Bullion store.

In the year of 1864 on December 3, the cornerstone was laid for the three-story Masonic Hall. Within this cornerstone was placed a zinc box containing several items relevant to the times and which, when tapped years down the line, would have to bring nostalgic smiles to all who perused them. Copies of the town's two newspapers, the *Mariposa Gazette* and *Mariposa Free Press* kept company with garden seeds, gold-bearing quartz and photographs of Abraham Lincoln.

The years from 1861 to 1865 were heavy with anguish for the nation, busy for Congress in a way that soon filtered down to both Mariposa and its close neighbor, Yo Semite. On June 30, 1864,

Yo Semite Valley and the Mariposa Grove of Big Trees were ceded to the state of California by Congressional Act. Cattle and flocks of sheep had been indiscriminately ravaging the wilderness lands. The Congressional Act defined from necessity, and as a result of these past and ongoing depredations in the Valley, the prohibitions to be adhered to henceforth. No person was to cut down, injure or set fire to any grass or tree, or allow their sheep or cattle within the designated areas.

In only the few years since Lafayette Bunnell of the Mariposa Battalion had first gazed over the magnificent vista, the Valley had been plowed and fenced, planted with grain and grapes and grazed by cows. Specimens of rare vegetation had been trampled and the stumps of felled trees left to mar the beauty of the place.

Naturalist and landscape architect, Frederick Law Olmsted, observed shortly after the Valley's settlement by homesteaders and hotel keepers that already hundreds of people were overcoming the difficulties of transportation in order to visit. Prophecy or wisdom, he went on to warn "before many years . . . these hundreds will become thousands and in a century the whole number of visitors will be counted by the millions." He was right on the money.

As providential as was the Act ceding this Valley of gracious beauty to the state, its consequences and implementation brought on the furies. Their holdings more than threatened, early homesteaders, James Hutchings and James C. Lamon, soon engaged in litigation to hold on to their homes and source of income.

It was a time of provocative change.

April 9, 1865

The war, which had shred families, split states and the country, and aroused the fiercest of emotions, finally ended at Appomattox Courthouse, Virginia, not too far north from where it had begun. Signatures ended the battles; nothing ever fully healed the legion of broken hearts or sucked dry the blood from the fertile soil.

3 Fire!

Transplanted New Englander John Jay Cook was a man invested with a go-forward bent and a visionary business sense, and after his arrival in California, he quickly invested his fortune in various enterprises, which he did not confine to Mariposa. He established a drug store, not only in town, but one in Merced. He became the Wells Fargo agent in Mariposa and then went further afield to San Francisco where he acquired part ownership in the well-known Taber Photograph Studio at 8th and Montgomery Streets. He then ventured into oil, buying interest in wells in the Santa Barbara area.

In a short time John Jay Cook and Henry Washburn became associated, and their lives were quickly interwoven in both a personal and business manner. John Jay became a financial advisor to Henry, who was himself of an energetic nature and possessed of ambitions for the future. With his wealth from his New York holdings, John Jay backed Henry in many of the latter's operations. He acquired a partnership in the Washburn stage line and soon purchased a quarter interest in land around the Washburn's newly-purchased Big Tree Station, a few miles south of the YoSemite Valley. Through his dealings in San Francisco, he met many of the prestigious and wealthy of that city and introduced his new partner to these illustrious people.

Sisters Jean Bruce and Fannie Bruce Cook were ladies talented in composition. Both had their poems published in the *Mariposa Gazette*.

In a town of emerging establishments meant to both knit and benefit a community, it is inevitable that the founders of those businesses should interlock. Henry Washburn met Jean Bruce, and from that time forward the business and personal lives of, not only the Bruces, Cooks and Washburns were interwoven, but soon the Van Campens as well.

December 18, 1865

This was an auspicious day. Mariposa dressed up for another gala event when Jean Lindsay Bruce married Albert Henry Washburn, thus uniting two of the town's most prestigious families. Henry was now related to the wealthy John Jay Cook as a brother-in-law and to John J. Bruce as a son-in-law. With the help of his new family, Henry would soon branch out into other fields of endeavor.

Jean Lindsay Bruce Washburn crossed a continent with her kin. She soon found her destiny and love in Mariposa. *(Bruce Family Collection.)*

The couple's first child was born January 21, 1867, but sadly, lived only one day. The baby, Henry Campbell Washburn, was buried in Mariposa's Odd Fellows Cemetery.

Their second child, Jeanie, born a year later on April 20, 1868, brought them happiness as she lived a long and productive life.

Too soon calamity struck Mariposa again, and the rebuilt successor to the washed-away Bruce

Albert Henry Washburn was a man of great insight. When he saw a need, he engineered a way to fill it. Those who knew him sang his praises.
(Yosemite Research Library.)

Machine Shop was square in the middle of that calamity. Life and times in the 1800s were chancy.

A fire struck on Saturday, August 25, 1866, started by a recently employed printer for the *Free Press* newspaper when he carelessly dropped a match after lighting his cigar. Flames and the yell of "fire" rose on the hot air at once, and the eastward-blowing wind immediately sent it past its origin near the corner of Main and 7th Streets to consume about 60 buildings representing $177,000. In one hour on a Saturday night, as the townspeople took to the surrounding hills to helplessly watch, the eager flames showed no discrimination. The summer-parched land and dry leaves offered impetus to its ravaging. If there was panic in this desperate time, there was also heroism as John H. Neale declared the *Gazette* office could be saved. Even then, flames were licking at the front and roof of the building, but Neale climbed to the roof and, with the help of Ben Cole, began battling the blaze

with buckets of water passed up to him. The building was miraculously saved.

Quickly claimed were the Methodist Church, the Odd Fellows building, the Masonic Hall, Terry's Stables, Schlageter's Hotel, a butcher shop, dry goods stores, saloons, livery stables, the Concert Hall and many homes. Among the latter was one belonging to the Van Campens. Left in a smoldering heap was the Bruce Brothers Machine Shop.

It was reported that during the conflagration all the dogs in town put up a big fuss, but on Sunday morning, not one dog howl could be heard. One more curious fact was later noted by the spared newspaper. Several Indians came into town, strode across the charred ruins and surveyed the damage with smiles on their faces. Perhaps they envisioned their land as once it had been and even hoped it would be again.

Although many townspeople despaired of having a town after this—its second devastating fire—rebuilding began while the ashes were still hot, and Sunday's despondency turned into Monday's rebirth of optimism.

Not to waste time, Peter Gordon quickly built an eight by twelve grog shop, dispensing the genuine beverage for a bit a drink. Schlageter made plans to immediately rebuild his hotel (this time a fireproof one) at the corner of Main and 5th; and on the corner of Main and 7th, Higman had his grocery store nearly completed. Farnsworth and Gallison put up their blacksmith shop, and a man by the name of Steinberger, who had earlier the same summer been burned out at Agua Frio, showed singular determina-

Daughter of Jean and Henry Washburn, Jean looks the fashionable picture of demure grace. Little could she have suspected the fight she would have in the future for the Wawona empire of her father.
(Roberta Bruce Phillips Collection.)

tion when he again hung up his sign **Boots made to Order.**

With a butcher shop built, the saloons swinging into action, a jewelry shop reestablished and a livery stable in operation, the town rose again. It had taken the determination and courage of these builders to give hope to those who had most despaired. And even though all the town's livery stables had been wiped out, Fisher's Stage Line became operational at once.

Aziel Barnes Van Campen made the most of a bad situation, even stating that the fire was of some benefit to him. He gained six months of full-time work making and hauling bricks to rebuild the stricken town.

Sadly, William Bruce died on November 25, exactly three months after the fire which destroyed his machine shop. He was only fifty-one. He was buried in the Odd Fellows Cemetery, up on the hill in Mariposa. After the fire, Charles Bruce took over the management of John Jay Cook's Mariposa drug store.

Though they had journeyed on different geo-

John Jay Cook was a visionary, an entrepreneur, and an investor. He was responsible for much of Wawona's and Yosemite Valley's commercial development. *(Bruce Family Collection.)*

graphic routes, the Bruce brothers' business routes and interests were often similar, even to being laced with misfortune. John had found opportunity with the Empire Stables, advertising the very best of livery horses and the newest and most fashionable buggies. On the other side of the world in Cuba, brother Robert Kale was involved in transportation.

Robert Kale spent almost his entire adult life in Cuba, always maintaining close contact with his family, for whom he held great affection and concern. In a letter to John Jr., he outlined the promising prospects of Bruce & Co.

> Puerto Principe
> May, 1867
> My Dear Sir,
>
> We take pleasure in announcing to you that we have established in this city a rail-road depot and also a foundry where we can manufacture and construct all kinds of machinery with the same perfection and at a less price than elsewhere.
>
> Those of our friends who think they can import from the United States with profit will find that we have ample facilities to make the articles here and give full satisfaction.
>
> This community has felt the necessity of this undertaking some time. Whenever a steamer meets with an accident to the machinery it has caused a great deal of trouble and delay for want of the proper appliances to repair it and a great deal of loss is suffered unnecessarily.
>
> Yours Respectfully,
> Bruce & Co.

Apparently the optimism of Robert Kale's letter either reawakened a sense of adventure in John or showed him the promise of opportunity, for he once more joined his brother in Cuba and did, in fact, become superintendent of the Nuevitas and Principe Railroad.

John Jay Cook had proved his business expertise since he ran away from the farm. When he saw opportunity he bought it. By 1867 he and Henry Washburn were partners in the Mammoth Tree Livery Stables, located on Mariposa's Main Street. In three years' time, he and David Clark took over the Lovejoy and Company Sawmill, and it became the Clark & Cook Sawmill.

4 The Scandal

Something happened in Mariposa. This time it was neither flood nor fire which caused the upheaval. A scandal forged in a fire of bitter words and accusations stirred the town and, oddly, bits of it sifted into the next century with Azelia Van Campen on the fringe of it by way of friendship. One of the main players, perhaps by no intentional design, was Adelia Seale, Azelia's friend of long standing and her faithful correspondent.

It began with the death of Rose Swaney. Her obituary was published in the *Mariposa Gazette* on March 2, 1867:

> Died—In Mariposa, Thursday morning, February 28th, 1867, Mrs. Rose Swaney, wife of A. M. Swaney, aged 24 years. She died on Thursday morning at her residence of Puerperal fever after an illness of ten days. There was scarcely any warning of the fatal character of her sickness, and this unexpected calamity falls with crushing weight upon the bereaved family, and strikes with surprise and sorrow the community in which she was so well known and so much esteemed. Mrs. Swaney, whose maiden name was Auburry, was born in Pittsburgh, Pennsylvania in 1843. She came to this place with her sister in 1859, where she was married to A. M. Swaney, the Editor and Proprietor of the *Gazette,* and where she has passed the too brief remainder of her happy, blameless and useful life. Her character was most unobtrusive, artless and domestic. The only ambition she seemed to know was to be a kind neighbor and a good wife and good mother. . . . The funeral procession will start from her late residence, corner of Eighth and Bullion Streets.

If Andrew M. Swaney wrote his wife's obituary, as he must have, being not only the paper's owner but the person who best knew Rose, there should be little doubt that he loved and treasured her.

And he would have sorely needed her continuing presence in his household to nurture the daughter to whom she had given birth only ten days before.

But Rose Swaney was not exactly to rest in peace.

On Tuesday evening, October 1st, 1867, neighbors heard the piercing screams of Adelia Seale. And four days later, the *Gazette* had another obituary to print:

> Died—At his residence in Mariposa, on Thursday evening, October 1st, 1867, of General Paralysis, James W. Seale, aged 44 years.

The obituary was written with the same praise of a high character that had been given Rose Swaney.

For the benefit of the circumstances, which crowded in upon this sad event, it should be noted that James Seale, an early pioneer of the community, who had come from South Carolina, was also a miner. He had recently returned from the Eastern Slope of the Sierra where he had been unsuccessfully engaged in mining operations. Adelia, his wife, observed that he had suffered several attacks of vertigo on the day of his death.

Perhaps there would have been no controversy, no wagging tongues to fuel further misery, had not the prussic acid, a highly poisonous gaseous acid, been found in the outhouse. With its discovery, Andrew Swaney and Adelia Seale were suddenly cast as murderers who rid themselves of their respective spouses in order to continue a romance heretofore unsuspected. The best of the town's tongues got busy.

Andrew Swaney was instantly put on a trial of the streets and soon forced to publish a rebuttal in his paper to clear his name after reading an accusatory letter printed in the *Stockton Independent.* He was bitter in his announcement;

TO THE PUBLIC:

Under the circumstances in which I am placed, it may not be considered by a generous public, criminal, unmanly or cowardly in me to address to you a few lines; not inc, defense of the grave charge made against me, for this is not the occasion, but simply to counteract to some extent if I can the unjust and cruel, not to say malicious, fabrications and exaggerations that have obtained circulation and are busily being circulated, to the hindrance of justice, the destruction of my character and blasting of all hopes for that impartial investigation of the charges made against me, that is guaranteed by the laws of this land to every citizen of the realm. It is sufficient on this occasion for me to say that I am charged with no less an offense than that of murder—that I am imprisoned upon that charge (though the imprisonment is to some extent voluntary on my part) and that I am innocent of that charge. . . .

His eloquent and vehement protest did little good to sway either the judicial system or the wagging tongues. Within a week of his bitter plea of November 4, 1867, both he and Adelia Seale were indicted for murder.

If Andrew Swaney felt bitter at the terrible turn of events in his life, Adelia felt betrayed that her beloved hometown could so turn against her. By June of the following year and before the case was resolved, she and her family left Mariposa for Stockton. She shortly wrote her dear friend, Azelia Van Campen, of her movements, her feelings and her intense desire to see her old friend. From the upstairs balustrade of her new home, she could see almost the whole city, though she was careful to write she never ventured outside to see the place or people and generally did not feel at home. She never mentioned if her sequestered life was due either to widowhood or indictment for murder, but she did allude with a bit of bitterness to the townsfolk of Mariposa.

> Write me, Azelia, who is the subject of scandal now, do people lie as much as ever? I imagine they have grown better since I left, do I accuse them wrongfully? I heard some nice scandal that was circulated here, but when I was told of it, Ma and I told them just what we thought, and that it was lies, it was about Mr. Irvin.

As much as her character had been impaled with poisoned stabs, as much as her morality had been assaulted, Adelia seemed to assemble her interests and thoughts with dignity, at least in her letters to her valued friend. Azelia was about eighteen at the time of the Swaney/Seale woes. Adelia wrote of fashions, how her fellow Stocktonians turned out for the Fourth of July procession, wrote of their property with its vineyard, peach, apple and fig trees, and of Miss Lizzie Kerr, who with her charming and captivating false curls, was suspected of being in town to look for a husband. And she was hungry to hear all the news of Mariposa.

But mostly she begged Azelia to come with her mother for a visit.

Azelia wrote in answer shortly after and her letter was read and reread many times, Adelia assured her correspondent. And there was a report Adelia felt compelled to rebut.

> Now in regard to the false reports, I will say a few words. I am at Ma's house and have been ever since I've been here, do not board at the Lafayette, and do not intend to. I have not been out riding with Mr. Swaney, or anyone else. I have not been outside of our own yard gate since we came here, do not believe I could find my way down town. So, Mrs. King is very much mistaken, she did not see me.

Spiteful words and accusations had followed the hapless Adelia far from home.

The troubled lady's spirits might have been somewhat bolstered by the new suit she made for herself. The fashion in dresses called for short in front with long trains. Her own was trimmed in black alpaca braid, the dress and sacque fitting very nicely, and was "nice for the dust."

In one of the few times she mentioned her stressful situation, she braved a measure of optimism when she went on to write: "I intend going out some after everything is over, which I hope will be soon!"

And it *was* soon! Certain to be prejudiced, the case with its sensationalism had a change of venue to Stockton, away from the worst of the viperous tongues. Swaney's attorney was Lewis Jones. He had been a close enough neighbor to the Seales that his daughter, Lucy, had heard Adelia's screams on the evening of her husband's death. The Stockton *Gazette* ran the story on August 7, 1868.

That city's District Attorney Pillsbury rose before presiding Judge Cavis in District Court and asked that the charges be dropped and the bonds under which the two accused had been held be canceled. To back his motion, he read a letter from the Mariposa Board of Supervisors, in part stating "we deem it but justice to say that we know of no newly discovered evidence which could strengthen the case of the prosecution in the Swaney case ... Therefore, in consideration of the facts as they exist, we would recommend that a *nolle prosequi*[1] be entered in the case."

Judge Cavis so ordered.

Oddly enough, Adelia, certainly one of the prime players on this judicial field and despite the fact she was living in Stockton at the time, was not to learn her freedom was a *fait accompli* for over a week, and then when she read it in the *Mariposa Gazette.* "I am glad I was saved the mortification of another trial," she wrote Azelia from Stockton. She had the faith of friendship with Azelia and offered her best wishes in the latter's career.

"I supposed that you had opened School again, as I saw in the Mariposa Gazette a notice that you would commence teaching again."

Two facts should have exonerated Andrew and Adelia, or at least been held in contention. Ten days before the death of Rose Swaney she had given birth to a daughter and contracted the dreaded puerperal fever, often invading a woman's body at childbirth and usually fatal.

However lethal the prussic acid found in Adelia's outhouse, however suspicious many desired to make it, the substance is used in mining and metallurgy, and James Seale *was* a miner by occupation.

It is likely that Andrew Swaney and Adelia Seale knew each other in the pre-indictment days. How well is conjectural. But if they were not acquainted with each other except in passing, or even as social intimates before their spouses' deaths, they surely had to become well-acquainted through both the ordeal of suspicion and the task of defending their reputations. Suddenly the two shared common bonds of indignation, worry and bereavement. And Andrew had a two-year-old daughter and a baby daughter to raise. So what they did next would fan the fires of doubt by those who yearned to doubt. They got married.

Further disasters were to put them on the edge of fear. Adelia spent at least part of a Sunday afternoon apprising Azelia of the news. It was March 21, 1869, and she was still in Stockton, though expecting to move soon to San Francisco.

It was the flood which rattled her most. More than the earthquake she had recently suffered through, she related, "just imagine yourself in a house where the water was within a few inches of coming in, and you could see nothing but water as far as you could see. Don't you think you would be frightened? I was terribly. We are afraid of having another flood yet, as it has been raining most all last week and the Sloughs are very high, and where we are living is a dangerous place near the Slough."

She was busy with household affairs, understandably so since in the house were three children to raise. Andy, she wrote, had given away the baby, Gertrude, to a Mrs. Webb, although without Adelia's consent. "But knowing as I do, that Gertrude has fallen in excellent hands, I am satisfied. . . ."

And despite the shabby treatment she had received in Mariposa, she had a longing for the old home! Then having thanked both Azelia and her mother for the congratulations they had sent, she signed herself as "Adelia Swaney." Andy sent his love.

Speculation and suspicion would occasionally flare up through the next century. Although it cannot be denied that Rose Swaney died innocent of her husband's hand, was Adelia Seale really blameless in the death of her husband? To what could his described paralysis be subscribed? The prussic acid? Could Adelia have had her eye on the successful Andrew Swaney? After all, her husband had just returned from the mines a failure.

In the long letters she wrote Azelia in the following years, she invariably begged her friend to visit and mentioned the illnesses she was so often suffering. Could the illnesses have been a form of retributive justice? The case may never be satisfactorily closed as long as memories linger in the minds of some.

---

1. The formal notice in law by a prosecutor in a criminal case that the case be dropped.

5 The Love Letters

Living in Hornitos at the same time as Azelia Van Campen was Albert Olcott Bruce, who had joined his brothers in the West in 1855. Their destinies were drawing close.

If Twentieth Century Hornitos, whose name means "little ovens," revels in its history and is prideful of the connotations of Old West ways, it is justifiably so. One story relates how the citizens of Quartzburg chased out an undesirable bunch of Mexicans who had begun filling up the town. The Mexicans established their own community of Hornitos.

Quartzburg, The Washington Mine, the Mount Gaines Mine, Quartz Mountain and Indian Gulch were all part of the same mining district. Today not much is left of those areas but memory, while Hornitos still boasts a dot on the map.

Somewhere between the Washington Mine, where Albert worked, and Hornitos or Mariposa, Albert and Azelia met.

The exact circumstances and date of their first meeting cannot be tracked, but it could have been at one of the frequent social events. It might have been the Bear Valley Ball on the Fourth of July, 1868, a Hornitos affair, or they could have been introduced by either of Albert's sisters, Mrs. Jean Washburn or Mrs. Fannie Cook. Both of these ladies were prominent on the Mariposa social scene. They could have met as they traveled between Azelia's school, Albert's Lodge meetings or family visits. Wherever it happened, a long relationship was spawned and a great destiny shaped.

Not content with her schooling acquired thus far or her beginning career of teaching school, Azelia traveled further afield. She returned to her studies, boarding in the comfortable home of a family with two daughters and two pianos at 626 Sutter Street in San Francisco.

Her parents sent money to cover costs of school, room and board. Summers were spent either in Hornitos or Mariposa. Later, she attended State Normal School in San Jose, graduating in 27 subjects ranging from art, music, and singing to higher mathematics. She began to sing with the San Francisco Opera Company, but surprisingly did not choose to follow that career. Perhaps romance was the motivating intervention.

In a still-existing letter from Azelia to Albert, she is informative, and in a sense, inviting. A sparked interest is obvious. She was then nineteen and he was thirty-two.

In a letter from San Francisco, dated July 30, 1869:

Mr. Bruce

Dear Friend,

. . . After several weeks of organizing and reorganizing of the school I have at last reached my destination in the third floor of an enormous building. The Denman Grammar School. I am very pleased with my school and especially with my teachers who are very kind to me and do all they can for my advancement which I appreciate very much. . . . The greatest victory is generally won by the most severe battle, what I get in my head can never be stolen from me. . . .

I hope you will not think hard of me for not complying with your invitation to come to the Mill. Uncle thought it would put him out so much I did not insist on his taking me over. . . . Mr. Washburn was down to the City since I have been here, but did not call to see me. I suppose he did not think I would like to see any of the Mariposans. I hope this will not be the case with you, if you come down this fall. Nothing gives me more pleasure than to meet my old friends. . . . I hope Fannie will come down with you. . . .

Azelia's mother, Harriet, was still in Hornitos, busy with sewing, giving piano lessons and tending to the duties the ranch required. She often called upon Azelia, living in San Francisco, to send up supplies. Often it was for dress goods for the ladies for whom she sewed. "Send her up a couple yards of white with fringe with a nice heading. Do it just as good as you can get for six bits a yard."

Grief could and did burden many. Not only was puerperal fever a scourge of the times that struck fear into any new mother's heart, but measles, scarlet fever and smallpox haunted the land. Little children would die so young. From Hornitos, on December 7, 1870, Harriet wrote her daughter,

". . . John Van Campen has come and called on me. The night he arrived I had a room full of company and no very good opportunity to talk with him. He says Eliza has had four children, two of them died with the smallpox and she came very near dying with it herself, but she lived through it and is not pitted. . . ."

Lean times assaulted these early pioneers, with only a lesser degree of burden than the diseases. Aziel Barnes (commonly called Barnes), in Hornitos also, wrote Azelia on January 1, 1871:

Dear Sister

. . . I have not wrote you in a long time. And we have not heard from you for sometime. Mother cannot think what is the matter with you. We are all well and wish you a happy new year. Howard is here. It is so very dry here we have had no rain yet to speak of. We boys find it hard to find work. I have not work in the shop for six weeks. I went and talk to Mr. Adams the other night, he wanted me for work as I did last summer—ten dollars per month and do all cooking, which is worth ten more. Little John and his wife is at Ira now. John is putting in the field on halves. I think he will lose all of it in the end.

Work was scarce, but Mother Van Campen has so much work she can not get time to write to you, she has to work Sundays and all.

Hard times knew no specific location and almost always paralleled the weather. In October of 1871, a letter was sent from Kansas, from C. B. Howard to his sister, Harriet, and it gave a grim review of hardship. There had been no rain to soak the ground in over a year.

". . . Cows last spring was worth from $50 to $70 apease. This fall the same cows won't fetch over $10. . . . Harriet, if you can read this you can do better than I can my eyes don't give the light they did when I was younger. . . ."

However busy Barnes declared their mother to be, she did find time to write Azelia.

March 12, 1871

My Dear Daughter,

I again sit down to write a few lines thankful I have hands and can write, but had much rather use my tongue to communicate with and hope soon to have the pleasure of doing so.
I suppose you are through those terrible examinations I hope your certificate meets your wishes. Mr. Brown says if you do not get a certificate such as you think you deserve if he was in your place he would go before the state board of examiners he thinks they would do you justice. I think you can get the Quartzburg School. I am unusually busy this week I have sent you thirty dollars by Express this morning you must get such things as you think best. . . .

From your affectionate Mother

Lean times were prevalent, but Azelia was always sent money for an education both she and her mother considered vital. This was somewhat unusual in a time when, if choices were to be made, the boys in a family were honored with the educational advantages.

Dances and balls lightened the humor and spirits. Barnes mentioned two or three balls at Hornitos, and one to be given the next night—January 2, 1871—at "Snelling."

And so the ladies had to look their best. Azelia was again called upon to make some purchases in the city and send them up by Express. One lady sent $2.75 with her order for a calico dress and a pair of Balmoral boots. Harriet instructed: "She wants a ten cent calico from Mosgroves. She wants nine yards of calico. If you can get her boots for a dollar, you can get her two dresses."

Two area masquerade balls were planned and the promise of these galas kept Harriet so busy outfitting the ladies that she once remarked to Azelia that she had no time to outfit herself for the ball.

Adelia Swaney became so ill that she was frightened she would die. Her husband, who she often referred to as "Andy" but just as often as "Mr. Swaney," did a little shopping for Azelia in this long period of his wife's illness. Whatever it was he purchased for her, Adelia was less than satisfied and commented "you know what a man is, anything a storekeeper tells him, he thinks it is right. I was afraid to send him back for fear he would make it worse."

The Swaneys were now living at 1003 Mason Street in San Francisco, while Azelia was back in Mariposa.

Harriet saw Albert from time to time, and the two were sometimes at odds, but she did confirm that he was courting Azelia. In a letter to her daughter dated March 24, 1871, she remarked that he was likely mad at her and referred to him as an idiot after he had made some remark about what he would do with a wife. Harriet thought him "so silly to converse with" and if she had offended him with her own remarks, she did not care.

At this time, Barnes was working as a blacksmith in Hornitos and by the following year, in 1872, he went to work in Merced for Sulerthern & McDonne. Brother Howard worked in Stockton.

By June of 1871, Azelia was teaching school in Mariposa and also seeing Albert on a semi-regular basis. From that time forward, there was no one else for either on the horizon of their romance. Love began to blossom.

There were love letters which were inscribed with growing devotion. Words to make poets smile and grandmothers blush. Albert was a poet and penned:

"... That you are mine, heart and body is enough. Your soul is too precious and belongs alone to God. ..."

"... Meet me with a smile, give me your thoughts and kind words and that is all I wish or dare to claim. ..."

"... Wish you were here tonight that I might plant one kiss upon your lips. ..."

"... Love and a thousand Kisses to you. ..."

"... Albert, I love you better than my life," Azelia once replied.

"... I still have that same love for you. Time had not diminished it but increased it.
"Yet come what may I expect to keep it till the day of my death. ..."

"... Life to me without you is worse than death, I would rather die a thousand times than to know we were to be separated for life."

Visits were not always easy, and the road of courtship often a rocky course. On March 8, 1872, Albert wrote from Hornitos "I came to town Tuesday Eve. in the hope of seeing you, but found my bird had flown. So had to trudge back."

So often, Azelia was the one who fretted at their long separations. "It seems to me that Sunday will never come. Tonight is Lodge night, but I guess you will not be in town, will You?"

From his place of employment, the Washington Mill, on November 5, 1872, Albert penned a long note to his sweetheart in which he mentioned that he was going to town for a twofold purpose. He was going to mail his letter to her and vote for Grant, both objects of importance, he assured her.

By this time their intentions toward each other were becoming more solidified, as Azelia wrote her dear Alberto (as she often called him):

Your happiness is my happiness, your joys are mine. It is only when I know you are well and happy that I feel contented. The tears of sorrow I have shed I hope may someday turn to smiles of joy when we will be together, enjoying ourselves beside our own hearth when peace and joy shall abide in our own cottage. Then I will be happy and be myself again. I care not how rude the dwelling or how humble the surroundings if you are only happy and content with me if you have my love and I yours in return. I hope never to give you one hour of misery or sorrow. I sometimes feel that you expect nothing but a life of misery with me. I fear your hope of future happiness has greatly diminished since you have become better acquainted with me, but I hope all may prove well yet and that I may be able to do a little something to brighten your life

Albert had expressed some curiosity about his family history. In a letter from John J. to his son, the father explained some of that background. A few words in the original letter have been smudged beyond recognition.

Mariposa 4th of Sept. 1872
Dear Albert

In your letter to Fannie, you said you never knew of any Scotch or Calcutta Property. The Scotch property is that on which I was born and to which I am heir to one half of proceeds. It was my mother's, where I believe she was born, came to my Father by marriage, was his children's at her death. My father continued to hold it for the benefit of his second Wife and her children. They held it while they lived, however unjust. That is the history of the Scotch Property it comes by descent to lawful heir and I am one of two left.

It is the bad practice of the world to retain all they possess to leave to their children by will. I would fain have something to give to help them whence I might see the good it did. If I had obtained a Legacy left me by my father but with it by my Step Mother it would have been some Millions difference in my favor today.

The Calcutta Property is mainly from Insurance and interest arose from the of ————my eldest Brothers Ship sailing between Calcutta and Madagascar. The owner and the Ships Captain, Charles Bruce, who was wrecked by a Cyclone and all perished but a Doctor and a boy.

Wished Father to send me out there. In 1809 by the laws of Scotland, I being his youngest Brother was his heir while by the Laws of England, My Father was. Nothing was ever done about it till last year a Scottish tourist bound for Yosemite undertook to enquire into it for me if his time permitting, which he feared it would not. Late in fall, I received a letter from Donald Graham, enclosed my Papers, Saying he could not devote to it the time required.

As Time had overtaken me in this journey through life without being able to distribute what I have left on Earth or which I can claim. Title which I design to bequeath to you and yours forever. Hoping you may succeed when you are————empowered and Instructed. This letter was written in such light I could not see to write or read. If you succeed in————Insurance and Interest on my Brother Ship it will make you the richest of all.

I must quit, I can see no more and my eyes hurt so.

Your Father
John Bruce

The informative letter proved that John still remembered Jennet well. And hardly with forgiveness for her finagling the property intended for his own mother's sons. He was seemingly resigned to that aspect of the property, but hopeful, too, that Albert might find a way to collect on the insurance from the ship's disaster.

From Mariposa on November 6, 1872, Azelia wrote her dear Alberto, chastising him for his errant ways: he had not written her for a while. (Actually, their letters crossed—he had written only the previous day.) Azelia had been helping Fannie make clothes for her children, and Fannie was to start for San Francisco on Monday. Then she became petulant. "I have not been quite so well lately. All on account of an old friend of mine deserting me I suffer." She went on to mention that Albert's father had sent a letter to Jim Lemon (most likely James Lamon, who had homesteaded in YoSemite Valley)[1] inquiring if that gentleman would be interested in joining him in building an oven to make bread for a living. "Seems to think he is a burden."

---

1. In 1908 the official and postal designation became Yosemite.

6 The Wedding

From the Washington Mill on November 8, 1872, Albert addressed the issue of his father feeling a burden when he wrote Azelia to tell his father it was "folly for him to attempt a business in Mariposa where no one can make a decent living and at his time of life he should rest and be comfortable. He has no reason to think he is a burden to anyone, any of his sons or daughters should feel proud to have him with them. I know I should. He is the representative of a past century. And has done enough in his life to satisfy all. . . .

"With the best love, I am your constant fellow, Al."

Adelia Swaney inscribed her friendship once again.

Something was troubling Azelia, and in a letter of November 12, 1872, Adelia was all sympathy, stating that she would do anything in her power to alleviate Azelia's suffering and implored her to visit in San Francisco, where she felt the climate would be good for her.

I might write pages begging and imploring you to come, but I do not think it necessary a few words from the heart will answer every purpose according to my ideas. If you will let me know I will come to Oakland and meet you, or if you cannot you can on your arrival take the Sutter St. car ride as far as Taylor, walk down Taylor to Post and up to 615. . . . Husband Andy is still working at the Alta.

Azelia never made the proposed trip which was to benefit her so much. She had other things to do.

Mariposa saw another wedding. Azelia and Albert proved their passionate words with a lifetime of devotion. They were married on December 2, 1872, in the parlor of the Schlageter Hotel by Rev. Dr. Clanton.

Present at the ceremony were:

John J. Bruce, Albert's father; Jean L. Washburn, Albert's sister, and her daughter, Jeanie; Fannie Cook, Albert's sister, with her three children, Jennie, Lizzie and Jay Jr.; Johnny B. Bruce, Albert's nephew; Katie Nichols, Johnny's fiancee; and the minister's wife.

Azelia's parents were absent. They had separated by this time, it is believed, and very likely did not care to chance running into each other. Her brothers were also absent, the likelihood being unable to take off from work since work was scarce.

Unfortunately, marriage did not end the couple's long separation. With Albert back at the Washington Mine and Azelia in San Francisco, their letters were the bindings that held them together as they consoled each other through the times spent apart.

Threads of humor sometimes laced Albert's letters to his wife.

I wrote to Stoddard today he will call on you be friendly and kind for he needs kindness—all poets do.

I think there must be a slip between Sam and his affianced. He came home last night hating all the world and declared if his enemies were only of the other gender he would pound them to jelly. . . . Sam concludes the course of true love never did run smooth. He talks of emigrating to foreign parts or pitching tent somewhere among the bogs of Merced City and there live and love in silence.

At the Washington Mine, a Mrs. Avord expressed her opinion of their separation when she told him: "It is all wrong that husband and wife should not be together. Why, Mr. Bruce, that's what people marry for to live together and be happy with one another. . . . You bet I wouldn't let my old man stay from me no nary time." To which Albert offered his own astute observation about the well-meaning Mrs. A. "Poor gentle female she hardly realizes that her hub is from her three-fourths of the time."

Azelia had returned to school, attending college at San Jose Normal. Albert was very proud of her when he wrote: "Do not think I sent you away for any selfish motive for if you continue in the mind to finish your Education all pecuniary profit of benefits belong to yourself. Mine the pride and delight in having you for a wife. And the pleasure derived in knowing that I have what few can boast a thoroughly educated one."

The couple was not in the best financial condition, and Albert insisted that in the future he would transact business by cash only and never again go into debt. In fact, he was ashamed of his indebtedness, begging his wife to be silent about it.

From the Washington Mine, he wrote of his desires.

> My Dear Wife,
> My heart desire is a little Cottage and five-stamp mill of my own and you with me then I will be happy. And if fate leaves me with health and strength all these I will get. You, I have got already. Providing no one runs off with you while below. Now Darling, I will close with true love from your affectionate bed fellow.

Azelia began to ail. Her mental health suffered as well since she did not hear from Albert as often as she would have liked. "I hope not in my hour of sickness when I need your love and attention," she beseeched him.

Her husband had his answer ready. "As for the improbabilities and impossibilities, I still doubt and told Turner to call upon you and find out what ails my old woman. To me the idea is too comical, a pretty looking dad I'd make."

She was not to worry about him, he assured her, for he was struggling to make a fortune for them both. "The self feeder I invented has been patented by a fellow in Tuolumne Co. I then invented another surpassing the first, and before I got my model even made I find it patented by two fellows in Frisco. I have invented a mill without stamps and amalgamator that beats all at present in use."

Albert possessed a great gift with the mechanical, but suffered the woes of many inventors whose work paralleled that of others at the same time, and who were first at the patent office.

A great sadness befell the couple. On January 8, 1874, their daughter, Elizabeth, came stillborn to them. Albert was at Azelia's side during this ordeal. Only a week later, a stricken Azelia wrote her mother and brother: "I regret losing the little darling much. It would have been a very pretty child, had it lived. I think it must have weighed nine or ten pounds, had dark brown hair an inch or more long, beautiful little hands & feet and little limbs and a Bruce nose. Was very plump and would have been a fine child had I carried it full time."

Albert was sent to San Francisco to negotiate for equipment for the Washington Mine. Azelia went along. He spent an evening playing cards and returned to his waiting wife with a slip of paper which was a deed to a piece of city property. Azelia decided they should check it out. The land showed no promise to them and the deed was torn up. Later, in 1875, William Chapmen Ralston built the 775-room Palace Hotel on that site. It was financed with money he had made from the Comstock Lode. The hotel became a congregation point for the wealthy of the country. Tours to Yosemite were offered from there. The Washburn, Cook and Bruce families would winter there and conduct various business interests located on Montgomery Street. This grand hotel was destroyed by the 1906 earth-

If the Belmont, Nevada courthouse was built to withstand the winds of time, it seems to have nobly survived. On a reconnaissance journey are Anthony and Michelle Phillips.
(Photo by Thomas Bruce Phillips.)

quake. Ironically, Bruce Mitchel Leitch, husband of Catherine Bruce Leitch, died there in 1888 while showing some of his paintings.

It was time to leave the Washington Mine. Albert was recruited for the position of Chief Engineer for the Belmont Mining Company in Nevada at $5 per day, but negotiated for $6 and was hired. He moved into the company house. His letters to his wife continued with frequency and love.

By the time he arrived at the Belmont Mine, its silver deposits had given wealth to some, hope to many and had, like California's discovery of gold, drained the surrounding area, like a thirsty watershed, of its populace. Six mines began operation, the Belmont the deepest at 500 feet.

A silver deposit had first been discovered in 1865, and within a few months the rush began. Mines, sawmills, newspapers and saloons quickly transformed the area into a bustling center of hopeful thousands. By the time Albert arrived in 1874, the town had declined, but in that same year enjoyed a resurgence of prosperity when rich, new deposits were discovered. In that year, too, the new brick Belmont Courthouse was completed.

Azelia stayed behind. Travel was rigorous, the distance great. They were separated again. But thoughts and letters traveled over the mountains.

Belmont Mine April 21st, 1874

My Dear Wife,

Yours of 16th inst. is at hand. Why are you unhappy? I should think at this time of all others you should feel contented. You know I came here alone for your future and good that all my struggles are for you even though it parts us for a while. I am in a fair way for success and eventually a fortune.

Though this County is cold and stormy almost constantly. Snowing even in summer months and anything but agreeable or healthy. Still I am willing to and glad to bear all to place us above want. Yes, darling, this will be my El Dorado, rest assured of that. I have little work to do, at least so far. Yet time goes on so that I will make thirty days per month. Webber's sending for me must have been an act of friend-

ship or pure kindness for there's plenty of mechanics here, good if not better than me. He could get for less wages if he chooses. I saw him yesterday for a few moments. He will post me if there is a chance to make anything on stock, so if I write for Henry[1] to invest he can do so without fear. Belmont town is about a mile and a half from here, a lively camp so I am told. I know nothing of myself having arrived at night and left for the mine in the morning, immediately went to work. As for the trip over here, you could not stand it at this season. Some of the distance you go on sleigh or an open box placed on runners. A barrel of water freezes solid over night. Speaking of water, it is a commodity worth coin, costing $1.00 per barrel, has to be brought a distance of about ten miles. From Battle Mountain to Belmont, you have to cross about 300 miles of alkali plains, changing horses every 20 miles, with no water to drink between stations. Austin is a town a little larger than Mariposa, supplied with hydrants on every corner to protect the place in case of fires. The revenue that keeps the place up is one mine and mill belonging to a New York company. Called the Manhattan Mill & Mine, they ship from 175,000 to 180,000 per month of silver bullion. I will write a better description of everything some other time. Above all, keep in good heart. Do not imagine my folks act queer to you. That is a mere fancy of yours. Any kindness they may show you comes from the heart. Jean and Fannie I vouch for. So darling, be cheerful in the knowledge that I am doing all in my power to make you happy and think of me as always near you if not in body in spirit and that I am your affectionate husband.

And as always, Azelia's loving and devoted husband signed with a dozen or so hugs and kisses, embellishing them with sketches of fluffy clouds on parade.

May brought no better weather. Belmont (its name means beautiful mountain) was cold. Albert probably enjoyed some surcease from the difficult environment with his letters home.

---

1. Most probably Albert's brother-in-law, Henry Washburn.

Even by the end of May the weather was engulfing Belmont with hurricane-like gales of snow and hail. Azelia wanted to join Albert, but he advised her against such a venture, writing that compared to the ride from Battle Mountain to Austin, "Fisher's (the Mariposa stage line) old jolt cart is luxury." He went on to tell her to go to school and take lessons in music. His dream was to save enough money for a small stamp mill. The dream for the gold helped him survive the harsh Belmont climate.

Two weeks later, on June 5th, in a letter to his beloved Azelia, Albert expressed his first show of disenchantment with Webber, the mine's superintendent who had first lured him to Belmont. It was over money. Albert had received only $186 of $196 owed him, and accused Webber of being at his old game of disallowing full time. Some of the rebel in him surfaced. "Today one of our boilers burst. Webber expected me to work all night repairing and this I refused to do. My salary being only six per day while other Chief Engineers get seven & eight—some as high as ten. The Old man thinks he owns me." But then Albert cautioned his wife to say nothing of his complaint, as he was grateful for his six per day, which was two more than paid in Mariposa!

Mariposa lost one of its esteemed citizens, one who had helped forge a future for his descendants in a volatile, rich and glorious land which held promises of adventure and enterprise. He had left his own mountainous region of Perth to ultimately discover another range of higher mountains in which he had thirteen years to enjoy. On June 17, 1874, John J. Bruce departed his adopted land. It is believed he was buried in the Bruce plot of the Odd Fellows Cemetery in San Francisco, where six-years later, his son, Charles, would also be put to rest.

Albert was distraught and gave vent to his sorrow in a letter to Fannie. He was certain, he wrote her, that "Father is far happier than on Earth, as he left it in true faith of an immortality, accepting and believing in doctrines of the purest character, his religion not founded on hypocrisy."

Apparently, Albert had escaped the excitement, the drama, confrontations and the ravages wrought by the occult and spiritualism, for he went on to tell

his sister what he had been doing on recent nights. He had felt it important to write a treatise of six or seven pages to confute her ideas on spiritualism, but then had second thoughts on sending it. He knew she was a believer in Christ.

Though both Fannie and Jean had experienced the intervention of spirits, such was not to affect them with the grief that brother, Robert Kale, continually suffered. The experiences of the girls were treated as a diversion rather than a threatening power affecting them. Such was not the case with their brother, Robert Kale. His suffering from the increasing influence of spirits left him devastated and too often powerless to fight back.

On the east side of Chowchilla Mountain, where once the Nutchu Indians had camped, Galen Clark was hard pressed to pay his financial obligations on his Clark's Crossing complex. For some relief of this intolerable situation, he took in Edwin Moore and his wife, Hulduth, as partners, and their way station for travelers journeying to the Mariposa Grove of Big Trees and the YoSemite Valley beyond was appropriately renamed Clark and Moore 's.

The partners were better hosts than businessmen and were beset with problems heretofore unanticipated. The opening of the Coulterville and Big Oak Flat roads on the other side of the mountain gave easier access to travelers and drew away much of their trade. Debts haunted them.

The Mariposa Book of Deeds in June 1875, recorded a significant sale. Clark and Moore's had been sold to Washburn, Chapman and Coffman and included all that had been built there--the lodging place, blacksmith shop, barn, sawmill and the bridge across the South Fork built by Galen Clark. Honoring the nearby grove of great sequoias, the complex was renamed Big Tree Station.

Henry Washburn had ideas of how to move into the future. With a clear idea as to how best lure the tourist to his new establishment, he began a wagon road into the Valley.

Despite the hardships of a particularly severe winter and with crews working from both sides of the proposed road, the 27-mile stretch was completed in less than five months.

Albert was still across the mountain range at the Belmont Mine. If Azelia failed to hear regularly from her "darling Hubby" she fretted. She worried that he worked too hard, that he suffered bad health or that some accident had befallen him. Their separation was almost intolerable for both, however much Azelia maintained that "the Laws of Divine Providence could not be improved on."

Her hubby was compelled to put her worries to rest by shortly asserting: "Are you not my Darling and Wife? . . . I am living and working for you that we may be together. You are my all. All I have to live for or cherish. No, Zeal, when I cease to think and struggle for you, I will also cease to breathe."

And then he gave her some cautionary advice. "If I were you I would not run after these paying mediums. They are too much like fortune tellers. So you commence to wonder and believe in Spiritualism, yet I remember the time you hooted the idea and your mother said I was a dunce to think there was truth in such things."

Although Albert had been describing the harsh climate, he apparently grew a bit defensive when Azelia mentioned what she had been told of it by another. "The lady that told you of this horrid climate was a humbug, and if she got her nipples frozen it was because she kept them uncovered." He did admit that the winter climate was not as mild as that in Mariposa.

Summer passed with Albert still at the Belmont and Azelia in San Francisco. She was planning to join him, but again he advised her not to make the long journey and risk becoming sick. "This country does not agree with me. I am loosing flesh and becoming prematurely old," he wrote her.

No chink appeared in their devotion. His health was another matter,

Weather and hard work were exacting a grave toll. Azelia relocated to Merced where his next letter found her, still urging her not to join him at the Belmont as the place had nearly worn him out. After a few hundred dollars had been accumulated, it would be goodbye Belmont. "I am failing every way very fast and suffer untold misery with neuralgia in head and back. I have some money to send you, but am too weak to walk to town after check."

Luck did not lessen his misery, for October still found him at the mine. His plans for a stamp mill of his own held firm in his expectations. "The thing fairly haunts me and I feel there is a stake in it for me," he wrote her. For some reason, he went on to admonish her to pay her board on time, as if she were staying at the E1 Capitan. Pride kicked in when he told her she may stay at that Merced hotel for a week or so should she so desire—for appearance sake! He would, upon his return, feel very small if he found she had not paid for a meal she had eaten.

Henry Washburn was now firmly entrenched at Big Tree Station where his wife Jean, reigned with elegant ease. She entertained presidents and other notables of the day, often with readings of her original poetry.

With a steady increase of travelers anxious to behold the special valley beyond as well as the close-by grove of giant sequoias, business demanded that Henry find better, more comfortable and faster ways for the intrepid and adventurous to enter the newly-acquired and growing complex. He needed to search out better ways for his guests to

Johnny Bridle Bruce was a partner in the Wawona Hotel from 1877 to 1882. Some said he was the smartest man in Mariposa.
(Yosemite National Park Collection.)

travel over the mountains, to procure supplies and advertise the accommodations.

These necessary demands upon him, he looked to his wife's nephew, Johnny Bridle Bruce. Johnny Bridle was the son of Charles and Mary Ann Bridle Bruce. He married Catherine Nichols, who hailed from Australia, as had his mother, and in time they produced three children, Fannie, Alice and Charlotte. He further intertwined the Bruce and Washburn families when, on March 7, 1877, he became half-owner of the Big Tree complex, paying $20,000 to Henry Washburn. Johnny Bridle and John Jay Cook then purchased a half interest of the stage line and stables.

Of the daughters of John J. Bruce, Fannie and Jean might have been cut from the same cloth, and likely velvet. Catherine carried her own unique vision of life. Upon the family migration to Mariposa, her husband, Bruce Leitch, became a Justice of the Peace as he had been in Williamsburgh, New York.

"I can say what few people can," Catherine once stoutly declared. "I have never worked." She elaborated on her philosophy. "If you never learn to do anything, no one can ask you to do anything for them."

Elizabeth Mary Bruce Auld was the daughter who stayed behind, choosing to forego the grand cross-continent journey to the West. Perhaps her husband was too well-established in the East, perhaps the rigors of travel too unappealing, or she just preferred her own known niche.

Both the Cooks and Washburns wintered in San Francisco when Big Tree Station settled down with only a handful of residents braving the deep snow.

Calamity took a stranglehold on the Van Campens. Azelia's brother, Howard, along with a Mr. Manchester, his employer, went hunting around the new railway-established town of Sumner, near Bakersfield. They were returning in a horse-drawn wagon when they stopped for water for the horses.

Charles Bruce sent the news to Albert. "While getting it, Howard let his gun slip and it struck the foot board and discharged the contents going through his heart and killing him instantly." Howard was only twenty.

In the same letter, Charles related another incident from a judicial viewpoint which may have expressed attitudes of the times. There had been another accident in which a local man was killed. Reports claimed the shooter was sent out of town for his own safety, but Charles laid down his own opinion rather bluntly "the most damnable lies, there is no doubt in my mind he has been lynched."

When the news of his wife's terrible loss reached Albert, he attempted to assuage her grief, and while all his letters were from the heart, this one offered a comfort expressed by words eloquent in meaning.

> Your letter of 11th inst. bearing the sad tidings of Howard's unfortunate death took me by surprise. I had been thinking so much of him lately. Laying out plans for the future in all of which he was to be concerned. . . . Darling, bear up under this affliction, think of our beautiful religion and feel that our boy is with us even now. Though you have looked upon the inanimate and cold house in which he was wont to dwell, believe he had merely changed. There is no such thing as death.
>
> And even now his pure Spirit smilingly hovers over you. God Bless him. He, with my relatives, has only gone before to pave the way and open wide the gates of Heaven that we may safely enter on our coming. Darling, you must not think him dead, by this time you surely know the good and pure never die. As I wrote this last sentence there came a succession of raps on the wall opposite where I sit. But I have become used to these things now living as I do entirely alone . . . . I will return soon as I can get money ahead to do something with that will make a good living. I no longer require to be rich to be happy. Very little will content me now."

And of courses he sent along kisses by the million.

Albert, despite previous skepticism, now acknowledged visitations from another world, but met them with a more placid acceptance than could his brother, Robert Kale. He knew that his steadfast devotion to God served as the contraceptive to harm.

According to the family Bible and substantiated by County records, Azelia and Albert's wedding date was recorded as being on December 2, 1872, but curiously, Albert recalled this happy day of his life as being on December 27. Could he have misplaced the date in his memory in only two years?

In the second year of their marriage, Albert was still at the Belmont, and on Christmas Day in 1874, he wished his wife a happy Christmas via the mail. "Day after tomorrow is the second anniversary of our marriage," he wrote, and then turned a little coy. "Do you regret it? Have I proved what and all you hoped for?" His own contentment with the marriage could never be doubted.

> Two years have passed over us, we are still poor. Yet I am supremely contented in my wife. We have sailed over a sea of troubles with adverse winds constantly sending us hither and whither where ever it pleases God it should blow. Death has come upon us and removed the aged and young. Our home has been left the charnel house of desolation. Do you complain or are you ready to accept the visitations of our divine creator on tended knee, and say Lord, thy will be done? Even as I write, I know and feel God permits his Angels to watch over me shielding me from harm. And if such as I am the recipient of his care, how much more so must you be.
>
> Try and impress this on your Mother's mind. It entirely removes the sting of death. Do not drape yourself in black. It is the badge of discontent. Go to his grave often. And there place the emblem of Purity innocence and faith in the form of flowers, white roses and lilies. . . .
>
> I hope this Christmas will find you happy in the knowledge that you have tried to do right through the past year. That you encourage no ill feeling toward any living soul. That in the moments of your happiest delight or the hour of your deepest grief you can look back over the vista of your married life without regret. All this is the prayer and hope of your absent affectionate hub. Here I sit upon a log of wood with a fire blazing beside me, writing on a bench. Alone, all alone in this desolate place yet am content because my body is only here. My mind and thoughts constantly with you.
>
> I feel poetical, so must get off some rhyme. It is the old feeling that returns when I am too much alone, a mania that tends to point to insanity. And when the spell is on one, always ends in a flood of rhyme. Good night, may

> heaven fill your heart with gladness. And forever shower upon you her choicest blessing henceforward from the approaching Christmas day. Love and kisses from your affec Hub, Al

Albert had a way with words. Had he not been able to express his deep feelings for his dear Azelia, his belief in God and Heaven and his acceptance of what he could content himself with for the future, it is doubtful he could have so staunchly borne the long separation from his wife. The release of his feelings in his continuing letters was undoubtedly a safety valve that helped his sanity in that miserable place. He belittled his need to express himself poetically by saying it pointed to insanity. It seemed, too, that he compromised his life's expectations after Howard's death. He was suddenly willing to settle for less than a fortune, perhaps acutely recognizing the frailty of life on earth. Clearly, he tried to discount the poet side of his nature rather than accept it as the great gift it was.

These years of 1873 and 1874 were Belmont's prosperous years with the town's population skyrocketing to 1,500 residents. *The Belmont Courier,* the town's newspaper was optimistically founded, continuing into the 1900s.

In early 1875, Azelia finally made the long journey to Belmont. It is unclear why she traveled over the mountains in what must have been the worst weather of the year, and after Albert had railed at it. A terrible loneliness must have been the motivating force.

And then profound sorrow once more struck the couple. Their second child, Robert, died on the same day as his birth, November 1, 1875.

Harriet Van Campen, alone and supporting herself, lived in Merced where she took in boarders. She bought a new organ and continued giving lessons. Somewhere along the way she changed her tune about Albert, for by March of 1875 she especially sent her love to him in a letter to Azelia.

October 22, 1876 saw the birth of Azelia and Albert's third child, Charles Howard. Concerned for the little one's health, Azelia moved to Merced to stay with her mother.

Albert left Belmont and, still interested in mining, prospected with Barnes. Thoughts of his wife and son were always with him. In January of 1877, he wrote Azelia that he and Barnes breakfasted on squirrel, the first fresh meat they had enjoyed in ages. There were two or three mines they wished to prospect before deciding if they would stay in the area.

February found Albert in San Francisco for a short time. He wrote his wife that he would not live there were he worth millions, and he longed to be back in the mountains. Why, he even preferred Belmont! Both Azelia and the baby Charles were suffering colds, omens whose seriousness he had yet to fathom.

Jean and Henry Washburn were wintering in San Francisco when, on February 17, 1877, Jean wrote Albert that she had seen *Camille*, and wished the lady in that performance would "adopt my play." Apparently, Jean was playwright as well as poetess.

Both Jean and Fannie despaired over brother Robert Kale's bouts with the spirit world and implored Albert to pray for him. Jean felt it was both dangerous and pitiful for Robert to yield his energies to evil spirits. From the tone of his letters, though, it seemed he was seized by these spirits, with no intention of yielding. His torment was intense.

By March, Albert was working at the Bullion Mine in Bodie, California. He never failed to write. Living conditions were harsh, the climate uncompromising, and his hands often injured with cuts, but he always managed letters.

My Dear Wife,

I was sorry to learn by your letter of a few days since that Charlie was unwell.

Hope ere this reaches you he may be well and lively as ever. The dear little darling—if anything should go wrong with him it would be almost death to me. You and my boy is all I have in this world to live for. And God knows my life is not of the happiest to be away almost constantly from all that is dear. . . . Am glad his grand mother is fond of him.

He is the hope of my life and the joy of us all. God bless my baby and keep him free from sin and all ills of this life.

Parenthood gave Albert an insight that prompted him to advise Azelia with eloquent and knowing words. "Let me caution you to be kind to your mother and show her every respect for remember you are a mother and know what yearning a parent has for her child. It is a love none other can compare. Be dutiful and obedient." It is doubtful that Azelia was any less to her mother than Albert beseeched her to be. Rather, that he had come to a fuller understanding of the depth of parenthood.

Azelia was with her mother in Merced during the baby's illness.

Always a miner with a dream of that elusive El Dorado, Albert finally hit the lode. He called it "The Bruce Ledge." But with the baby ailing, he had no time to file a claim, and a man by the name of Clarence Mackey jumped the claim and within 24 hours had uncovered the largest clump of gold ever found in one chunk. It weighed 21 pounds.

Heartbreak hit Azelia and Albert again, and again, dreams died. Little Charles was barely five months old when he died on March 16, 1877, but he would never be forgotten. His father spoke of "Little Charlie" for years.

Later, in a letter begun only "My Dear Darling Wife," Albert wrote:

We have consecrated the earth with the blood and body of our children.

Three little graves and three Angels in heaven. God bless you and lend strength to bear this last and greatest of all afflictions. Our darling is in heaven protected by the eternal watchfulness and divine love of my mother. God afflicts to draw us nearer to him. Our child was but a loan from the Angels. They could not spare him long. And have taken him home. This darling is the link to bind our hearts closer together. Let us unite in prayer that after a little while we may be permitted to join our family of Angels. My whole body and strength of life was centered on our boy. Had I no belief in the grand reunion of all on the other shore, the blow would be unbearable.

After continued words of both faith and resignation, Albert hinted of an insight he held when he told Azelia:

Mother was with me last night and I was transported to Fannie's house. She wanted me to do something to relieve Fannie's mind from anxiety of some kind, what I did not learn, yet knew something was wrong, and what was it the death of our babe.

I hope you will bear up under this bereavement and take consolation from the knowledge that our babe has only changed form and awaits us on the other side. . . . I almost think I can hear him cooing and laughing as he did before I left him.

Azelia answered her husband's mourning with words which expressed her esteem of him. Referring to his lost riches, she wrote: "Any other man would have hired a squaw to keep house. Our real loss was Charles."

The Bodie cemetery, on a knoll above town, bears witness to the fact that many died young. *(Thomas Bruce Phillips photo.)*

Albert went back to the Bodie mines. If the weather was harsh in Belmont, Bodie could brag of an even worse climate. Bodie is located in the high desert, 12 miles north of Mono Lake, and in 1878, it was the second most populated city in California. In sin and violence, it probably had no rival.

Bonanza Street, one of the main drags, was also called the Street of Virtue. Many of the town's single women took residence on this street. By dint of their profession, prostitution, most died young and were buried in unmarked graves to be forever forgotten.

Residents cared for one another, helped one another, and while most yearned for law and order, a few created the law's disorder and almost always

got away with it. Violence reigned as prime contender to life there, with murder unpunished. Opium addiction and suicide were the leading ways to relief in this culturally austere place.

Along King Street on the northeast side of town, a Chinatown flourished with the selling of fish, chicken and pork. And that most valuable of commodities—firewood. In that tree-barren place, firewood was brought in via long lines of donkeys until The Bodie and Benton railway was established in 1881 for the prime purpose of hauling firewood. It carried no passengers.

Lodging costs were prohibitive, and Albert slept wherever he could, for a time with an old Mariposa friend, Billy Irvin. He worked at the Bullion Mine, later called the Standard Mine. This mine and the Bodie Mine were the last in town to survive the grave mining slump which left the place a virtual ghost town by 1883.

Despite the expense of living, the harsh conditions and the uncertain prospects, it was related that a friend in Bodie was a friend for life. There reigned a youthful enthusiasm, a feeling of freedom and a wonderful sense of expectation.

Ultimately the town was to die a death as cruel as it had lived. A fire started in a kitchen in 1892 and destroyed 60 buildings. The final death knell rang in 1932 when a fire did in most of the surviving town.

Albert's time there was full of his own stress. He was often sick and had to keep rags on his painfully cracked fingers. He was, as always, anxious to save money and get out of town, for: "A winter in this place would kill me. Summer is bad enough."

Prosperity was still in the cards when he wrote from the Standard Mine on June 5, 1877.

Our new mill will be ready to run about the first of July. We have been grinding at a custom mill of 16 stamps. Last week cleaned up $21,300 for six days run. When both mills run we'll ship $100,000 per month of gold. Think of that, for men who were once poor as myself, there had been money enough taken out since I have been here to pay for mine. $75,000 for mill, $45,000, and about $2,000 per day working expenses and more. The Cook Bros. and Johnnie Boyed have all clear, just like finding millions in the street.

Within a month, Albert's own worth was reflected in another letter to Azelia:

I am very busy working late and early, acting as Head Machinist for the mill contractors by permission of Billie Irvin. I have quite a reputation as a quick and good mechanic, better than at Belmont, and the mill builders have had to call on me to finish up things. We have a machine shop attached to mill and I am to have charge of all, a better position than I have ever held, even if I do not get a very large salary, but we are in California not Nevada now.

Ah, Bodie. If only it had lived! Today the town looks weary and defeated, but once it bustled with commerce and a lot of hope. *(Thomas Bruce Phillips photo.)*

Big changes in their lives were about to be. Although he hoped to leave Bodie in August of 1877, he suggested to Azelia that she go to Mono Lake and then ride on to Bodie, only 12 miles distant. By the following May, he was thoroughly discouraged, having left Bodie after a presentiment of losing his life. "I had my arm broken there and worked continually with the bones grating together."

It was probably Fannie Cook's letter that changed the course of Azelia and Albert's lives. Fannie was on a visit at Big Tree Station when, on June 16, 1877, she penned a note to Azelia, still with her mother in Merced. Fannie begged her sister-in-law to escape the heat and come to the Station. She also voiced a minor petulance that her own short stay there was not particularly happy. The problem was that Henry Washburn had left for a time, undoubtedly on one of his many business ventures, and left his wife, Jean, to the running of the place. And Jean was kept busy. Nevertheless, Fannie suggested that Azelia go to the mountains. "I, of course, don't pretend to give invitations to any though I have a right, if money makes it."

Fannie was conscious that, though she played no active role in Big Tree Station management, her husband's money had made it viable. Although Jean had been too embroiled in the myriad of hotel duties to give her sister much attention, Fannie's slight was some eased with a trip to the Valley where she spent some time at Barnard's Hotel. She went on to relate: "Agent made the world of us taking us around in a carriage. I shall remember them for it, and pay they would not take."

The short Valley excursion was a tonic Fannie badly needed, for there was fighting among the employees at the Station, leaving her with major annoyance rather than the bliss she had expected to enjoy. Still, Fannie insisted, she was sure Jean would rejoice in having Azelia stay there.

Azelia accepted the invitation. Albert's feelings about the move were ambivalent. He admonished his wife not to work her life away for the comfort of others, and if things do not look so favorable there when he arrives on the scene, why, he will take her away! On the other hand, he wrote her, he had spoken to Henry Washburn and would probably work there as a blacksmith. "Anything to be with you. I am distracted."

The happy times began.

7 Letters from a Distant Land

As much as Azelia and Albert's marriage was filled with love and devotion, Robert Kale and Jane Bruce's union was filled with discord. To flee this unhappiness, as well as accord Cuba with the needed growth materials that his genius for the mechanical could supply, Robert Kale decided to call that country his home. But if marital discord at home caused him to abandon his homeland, the place to which he fled very nearly brought about his demise. His brush with Cuba's history almost painted him out of the picture, as attested in a letter written to his sister:

Pro. Principe Sept. 6th, 1871

Mrs. J. L. Washburn

When communication was cut off from Naurtas, Havana by the rebels, I left utterly destitute and my business and properties ruined, and had to fly to the Country and live with the insurgents to get food to eat. A few days before the Town was relieved I returned to town, and was arrested as a spy and accused of making cannons outside. And would most certainly have been shot if some powerful friends had not interceded in my behalf and procured my release. When the Spanish troops proceed their way from the sea to this town and saved us from starvation was the time my services were required to get rail road matters in running condition. I was the means of saving many lives and the R. Hood Company from incarceration. Have since remained in their employ at a salary of $204.00 per month in capacity of Civil Engineer and Master Mechanic. And my services fully appreciated both by them and the public.

Remaining your Affec. Brother
Robert Kale Bruce

Politics, history, suspicion and the Spaniards had a way of altering the life of Robert Kale. Even though he had long established himself as useful to Cuba's economics, he was required to take a sort of sabbatical from that country and his varied interests there.

Interestingly, he first seemed at peace, perhaps even enthralled with the "gift" visited upon him. The spirit world had not yet victimized him completely, but its beginning was in evidence.

In a letter of September 18, 1874, he wrote to his sister, Jean, from Brooklyn. Jean was then at Wawona/Big Tree Station.

Dear Jean,

Lib says that you have requested that I write to you. Well, God knows I have plenty of time at present.

First, I would say that it would afford me pleasure to learn of your good health and propriety and all those connected with you in that distant land.

Second, that our humble servant is a wanderer from the ever faithful and verdant Isle of Cuba. The Spaniards supposing probably that the air of that flowery land was deleterious to my political health kindly requested me to seek the more bracing atmosphere of Vespucius land. The change has been for the better in a sanitary light but not financially speaking.

I have worked some since my arrival but find that I cannot stand the hard labor of a machine shop and the consequences is that I must return to Cuba or seek some other climate as genial. Parties have made arrangements with me to go to Cuba again at Cienfuegos to run off a crop and I leave here in ———. There may be another chance to go to Venezuela. But to be frank, a dread seems to seize me at leaving this country again. My interests demand this sacrifice, and it may be never to return.

I should go to Calif., but from what is told me matters there appear to be on a par with N. Y. I am a strong man yet and am fast regaining perfect health, but should necessity compel me to return South again, maladies will accumulate again as usual. The tropics of the West Indies do not suit Northern constitutions. Tis a slow way of committing suicide.

Since my return to N. Y. have been amusing myself by the scientific investigation of spiritualism and have seen most wonderful and strange things and have developed considerably myself so that the spirits speak through my vocal organs, write fluently and beautifully through my hands and answer Sealed letters, if brief, by they say that I am destined to become the best medium in the county by development. The seances at Lib's are very fine and at other places where I have attended truly marvelous. If it will bring good to me and assist me to a point to good to humanity then I will give it more attention. If not, why then I think of doing right. . . .

As this paper is diminishing in space will close with kind love to all. With the assurance of your accepting the same.

Remain your loving brother
Bob

By 1876, the geography of his life had changed, as had his attitude and regard for the spirit world, which he now understood meant to harm and destroy him. He was a man beset with pain and a deep wretchedness of the soul. He wrote to one of his brothers, probably Albert, who was then in Belmont, Nevada.

Dear Brother

For twenty odd years I have been molested by spirits from the time that Jean and Fanny sat with me at the table to investigate. Every misfortune that has befell me since. And also to all the members of my Father's family can be attributed to this cause. I now know that the crushing of my skull at Bruces was part of their revenge. And may be all my misfortune previous to that. I have been lured on by their influence and impressions in my whole subsequent career, believing that the investigation would result in good. Tis sufficient to say that they have gained their ends by threats and influences best understood by invisibles alone.

If I have erred in my life the mistakes have come through them. Because I was not myself, but merely an instrument in spiritual hands. And my gain has been family discord, the death of children and myself made unhappy and miserable.

All that took place at Auld's I am innocent of. We called around us spirits bitter and relentless enemies of our family whose object was to destroy the intellects of my children and injure those of Mrs. Auld, and they succeeded as the state of my children can bear witness. My acts in boyhood as after life may be somewhat the cause. But have I been a free agent. Emphatically NO! Obsessed to gratify the passions of devil or used as an instrument to flight—my own prospects probably bring trouble and misfortune upon others.

All this have befell from boyhood even from the cradle, born a medium and since developed to a degree Which I would God had spared me. Or had let me die in the cradle that was rocked by spirit hands.

The worst of my afflictions date from my marriage and the vengeance of Jane's Parents had followed me ever since, and I feel her Father's presence has been my bane, and in committing offence against me has also ruined his own daughter. What must have been this man on earth, He must have been bad, as he could not have thus injured human beings as he has done me simply for the reason that in his mating us, he failed in calculations to secure <u>his</u> own salvation and happiness in the other world.

I am now obsessed by his spirit completely obsessed and made to suffer. If God had only kept me from meeting that woman again. And the revenge and malice of her Father so implacable both to me and mine. . . .

I am working but tormented continually, and every effort made to spoil my work and depreciate my merits with my employees. And drives me from pillar to post. Thus have I lost good chances and all my money.

How this spirit deceives other spirits God alone know, but he makes them believe me a fiend incarnate as was done to the spirit of Auld both in Cuba and New York.

This must end and the only way is to read this letter there in California so that all our friends even to my Father and brothers may hear it and come to my rescue before they kill me as they are doing in every conceivable way. All this seems strange to you, but nevertheless true! That we are allied to the spirit world in body and soul and that this spirit uses my facilities at pleasure and would lead me to do wrong again but a higher power restrains him and my own moral will sustains me. Thus far I can conquer him, but in petty spite and low malice lies his power to injure me at present.

Hundreds of spirits come to me, some for good and more for evil. But the good must predominate in the end and I hope by the life I now lead to be free. Still it may be by death, but with God's help, and prudence on my part I may be spared to do much good yet in the world. . . . I forgive the part played on earth by Jane. But I do Not wish to meet her again.

So I have been the innocent cause of trials and suffering to my Father's family much because this spirit believes they treated his daughter with indifference and scorn. But how mistaken was he had he reflected that she would have been welcome to all. And now have had a happy home by my labor and her children. . . .

I now make if God spares me this Island my home, amidst those that will be my friends, providing this evil spirit leaves me. If not, and one comes to my rescue from Calf. I will go there even if it is to run a locomotive upon the plains. . . .

I write this hurriedly, and hope it will bring the relief which I feel can only come from there.

From these remarks you can now know Who has injured our family and is injuring me. And turns both this and the spirit world against me. And had it not been thus, this day I would have been wealthy and respected by all. He is the author of all with the assistance of those that follow him. And all mistaken in supposing that the evil comes alone from me. One demon like this spirit would upset even the spirit world if allowed to act there as he does with me.

Give me your opinion on this letter and believe that all I write is true. Because they dictate more of it than myself.

Hoping to hear from you soon . . . with good wishes to you and family.

Your affect Brother R.K. Bruce

Robert Kale's life, with its miseries, triumphs, concerns, and heartbreaks, is laid out in his letters from Cuba. It was a life as tumultuous as that of his adopted country, but Cuba eventually rested with more tranquility than did Robert.

The most benevolent judge would have been hard put to ease Robert's path through the trials that plagued his life. Before leaving the United States he had entrusted the care of his daughter, Jeanie, to a Mrs. Auld, and thereafter sent money for her keep. Jeanie, much like her father, was not to have a happy time. After some misunderstanding with the Aulds, she left their house. She was an attractive young lady and might possibly have posed considerable competition with suitors for the Auld girls in the household, her father often felt.

Jeanie's life took a tragic and irrevocable turn. Having removed herself from the field of marital competition at the Aulds, she married and divorced. But it was not the discord in her marriage which was to most trouble her. It was in 1875, on one of her father's visits from Cuba, that the totally unexpected changed her life around. Robert suggested a small diversion of Table Tipping. (Table Tipping is similar to a Ouija Board in that it may invoke spirits to come out and communicate with the living world.) Within 15 minutes, Jeanie was controlled by some influence or some spirit and could never divest herself of the presence which seemed to obsess her.

Jane, her mother, forced her into an asylum, and thus the sorrowful and tragic years began. Confinement rather than help was all that was given her. Robert was certain that good magnetic treatment by a thoroughly developed medium would restore his daughter to her former self and sent money for that restorative process, but the treatment was never effected.

It was perhaps Jeanie herself who could have flung open the asylum doors had anyone listened closely enough. By this time Galen Clark's little stopover, Clark's Station in the Sierra, had been sold, evolving into a hotel complex and renamed Wawona. With several Bruces now in the area, Jeanie wrote her Wawona relatives, beseeching them to allow her to come for a visit to soak in the splendors of the Yosemite Valley. She was certain that walks in the woods and singing nature's tunes would heal her body and spirit. Strangely, no one seemed to hear the clarity of her words and mind as evidenced by her lucid thoughts.

As she had feared, her plea to visit California was ignored. Wives did not fancy female cousins around. It was the Auld story all over again.

In addition to his despair over his daughter, Robert's own health was on a downward spiral. He, too, voiced his own wretchedness and continually wrote letters to his relatives pleading for any help or cure they might offer.

Gift or demons, visionary or victim, the times allowed no latitude in judging Robert's further tortures. His spiritual well-being came under constant attack from influences unidentified. He suspected he was an unwilling medium to the underworld. Both visions and voices haunted him. He spoke of beds being lifted off the floor and the spirits invading his body.

It is not too difficult to imagine the many indignities suffered by Jeanie in an institution freely called a lunatic asylum, but perhaps incomprehensible to fully understand the degradation she endured during the years of her incarceration at the Flatbush Lunatic Asylum.

Although the doctors pronounced her incurably insane, Jeanie wrote from behind the confines of this institution with words that spoke eloquently and from a mind forming lucid thoughts, observations and plans. Her letters were cries for help, but they were addressed to relatives on the far side of the continent and went unheeded. Perhaps had her father's business not kept him in Cuba, and he had not his own demons to battle, his own despair at her condition could have been rerouted to offer her the aid she so desperately sought. He seemed powerless to help beyond his grief for her.

Evidence of his anguish at the spirit world's hold on him continued in a letter to sister, Fannie:

April 27, 1880

Dear Sister

The last word from you was written on Nov. 14th, 1879. . . . In said letter you stated that Charles was very ill, and had undergone dreadful suffering for many months. A few days past, I received a letter from my daughter Katie who stated that my brother had died, glad to go, be relieved from his terrible

suffering. It is surprising to me that no word has come from Cal. notifying me of his death. Of course, I think but that you have written and the letter lost in coming. I regret deeply that Charles has left this world without one word to me, maintaining a silence of over thirty years, and for what cause I never could fathom. But I have the satisfaction of knowing and feeling that in my heart, there never existed one thought against that brother, nor do I believe that he entertained any thing against me, and as for this silence, I feel was simply mutual reticence. . . .

In or about the 5th of February as I stood talking to a friend, a voice spoke to me clearly, these words, Your brother Charles is dead! Twice was it repeated, and we marked the date. While lying very ill with bronchial affliction about the 15 of March, received word from Katie as mentioned.

Do me the favor to tell me when did this event take place. Several times has this horrible obsession notified me in this way, and it always has turned out to be the truth.

Charles had died on January 19 of that year.

Robert went on to request she tell their brothers, Albert and Johnny, to write to him of all they were doing and if happiness and prosperity had touched them. He would have enjoyed seeing both her children and Jean's, he told her, along with the wish that they be well educated with the advantage of prestige and position in society. Then Robert again mentioned the spirit world he could not throw off.

You may remember a slip of paper I sent many months ago, a doggerel rhyme written by a spirit. That paper was written by Mary Rice, our aunt and the wife of Uncle James, who in spirit has followed me and caused me every misfortune and calamity in her power to inflict. The paper was sent not to recognize any merit but for you to acknowledge the expression of vengeance that lingered in her heart against us as she has often stated to me, for the contempt of our family (s) his and hers, and for the mistakes of my life in giving evidence in the trial against her. That woman had no advantage of education, nevertheless, she has used her power against us and has caused us misery and suffering from the invisible world, not even stopping? You may ask how I know all this. I have seen the proofs, am a medium against my own will, I see, hear and feel these invisible beings (for this world), have walked and talked with them, have placed paper upon the table and their perfect photographs have appeared without human agency or instrument of any kind and amongst people that never saw me before, nor even knew my name . . . even to the veritable Mary Rice, free from her pock, marked face, bearing a calm placid triumphal countenance, handsome, almost to believe that vengeance lurked beneath its spiritual expression. From this intercourse with this world, I fell into the powers of their will and mind, the result you may behold in subsequent misfortune, Jeanie's obsession and sufferings and a knowledge given to me of intuition, laying bare the consequences of all the past, not only to myself but to you all and proving that evil followed us. . . . Thus does the invisible world create dissension, discord and suffering to those they hate, throwing aside all hope of progress in their efforts to carry out the dictates of their natures that cling to the spirit . . . leaving this world undeveloped. Anyone that dies without education never can leave this sphere until God blesses them with a balanced mind and intelligence derived from intermingling with mortals who have the advantage of culture and intellectual improvement, for this reason penalties should be inflicted on those who neglect to educate their children, for in this effort lies their happiness and progress in the future state. . . .

You ask me to assist Jeanie. I am doing all that is possible to this and can assure you that she can be cured, but only by the power. . . .

What you say of your husband I know to be true, you are not the only one that has praised him to me. His whole life has proved him to be an honest, upright and worthy man. . . .

Sincerely yours,
Robert Bruce

Although Robert understood not only who plagued him but the methods used to steal his peace of mind, he was powerless to stop this dreadful intervention. He was a man beleaguered with frustrations and agony.

Physical problems, as well as the mental, plagued him with such relentless pursuit that it is remarkable he was able to manage the awesome duties of his employment in Cuba. He often wrote to Albert, begging for some word of cures for his various disorders. And always he shared his terrible ordeals with the spirit world which never allowed him rest.

How many times I have tried to give you full details of all that I have passed through, but have been crushed down by spirit power who have almost ruined my mental faculties in their opposition to my attempts. . . . They bring evil and retard the progress of everyone that falls into their power. My history with them would fill a volume and my body is obsessed at all times and brain impressed day and night and bodily torments by their power that would drive men of less nerve and firmness to suicide.

In the same letter to Albert, Robert expressed the wish that he were rich enough to make a flying visit and see the beauty and grandeur of that wonderful country.

Despite his desire, he was never afforded that opportunity. In fact, there is no evidence that the brothers were ever to meet again once they had taken their separate paths from New York.

And the worst had not yet traveled through Robert's life. On November 6, 1895, he wrote a disturbing letter to Albert, with whom he was sharing a violent page of history:

Dear Brother,

Since writing you last, we have been in the midst of catastrophes. The insurgents are continually infesting our R. R. lines. Beside burning villages and Stations, have now commenced the use of explosives. Blowing up bridges, culverts, locomotives and trains with Dynamite bombs exploded by electric wire from apparatus in the woods. Three locomotives have been hitched from the train and terribly injured. The last one on the 26th of Oct., the engines and two firemen being literally torn to pieces. With serious injury to passengers and employees. These assassins are the most vandalic devils that ever walked the earth, some of them being men and apprentices from our own shops. They make no discrimination whatever and would kill their own brothers were they adverse to the cause that they uphold. We are not the only sufferers. Most of the Railroads on the Island have been subject to this horrible and inhuman vengeance. You can imagine what work we have to keep this line open. The losses to this Company have been immense both in Engines and Cars and material of the road. We are cutting down the woods and brush 500 metres one each side of the road way a distance of 45 miles. This precaution will allow the troops to inspect along between the forts each morning before the trains pass. The small forts contain 25 soldiers each with Lieutenant and subordinate officers and are one kilometer apart. Nevertheless the rebels seem not to mind these preventatives. And in several districts have compelled the troops to evacuate or surrender their strongholds. Their system of warfare is very harassing, to the troops, having the advantage of the woods for retreat and ambuscades. And do sometimes attack convoys on the open roads and have captured much war material in this way. A more relentless and heartless set of wretches never existed, outrivaling in wickedness the Musselmen in their massacre of the Armenians. All of this springs from their deadly hatred and jealousy of the Spaniards. Exhibiting the same sanguinary nature possessed by the descendants of the Latin race.

This war is destined to be a long one. Even though the Cubans were granted "Autonomy" they would never be satisfied. They seek independence.

But from what I see and know of the Castillian character, their efforts will be futile. Of course, the Island will be ruined, but Spain will remain the Master even though she sacrifice her last man and last dollar. I prefer Spanish rule. She has well constituted governing power, and the right of her discoveries. The Cuban pretensions are based on no solid foundation, and their ignorance most profound, except in a few cases of men whose enlightenment was acquired in other countries civilized and advanced in knowledge.

I have written that you may just know how affairs are in this "Never faithful Isle," and should things become worse or better will keep you apprised as circumstances will admit or permit. . . .

After signing in his usual fashion of affectionate brother, Robert Kale again mentioned the troubling personal aspect in his life. Though he was powerless to rid himself of the threat, he had gained an insight. "I have matter for many pages on occult affairs which would require more time to indite than I have at my disposal at present. Between my duties interior and exterior occupies my undivided attention. Still I know that every event occurring is from an ultramundane source, which is guiding and reeling through every atom of life in every form imbued with intelligence, will and action, both for good and evil according to environments of each and every one born into the world."

Resolute as he attempted to conduct his life, brilliant with the mechanical, visionary in business, Robert was powerless to stop the invasion into the chambers of his soul and cast away the spirits who sought their vengeance. He named them explicitly in one of his outpourings of sorrow and despair. "The object of Spirits towards me is to humiliate me, prevent me from succeeding in life and if possible to make a pauper of me and mine. Could any family have remained together in harmony no power could have injured us."

Then, in one of his long and explanatory letters, a shocker. His brother, John, was a victim of the spirits. Had they known how to channel these unruly and persistent forces, it is possible good could have come of what Robert considered an affliction. Perhaps his adversaries could have been turned, much like the spy who changes sides.

Robert was growing older; he was in his late seventies when he wrote sister, Kate, on January 1, 1899. California was still on his mind, though by now he realized he would never get there.

I never would have started for that distant Section of the world without being fully equipped with all requirements. I have "paddled my own canoe" since boyhood and will continue to do so until death closes my eyes.

My intention of going to Cal. was premature although I am sure that I would have have had employment at once as my letter of recommendation were from the highest sources and to the highest individualities. . . . I am known from Cape to Cape in this Island and my reputation is unsullied by any act that could hurt my social position and my mechanical ability above the average in my line, both theoretical and practical, including experience in commercial affairs.

So you can assure my relations to be in no way embarrassed in anticipation of a visit from me. I would have liked to see my nearest kin once more, but as matters have changed in the Island, must forgo this pleasure.

He became rather stiff with a pride which, despite allowing that he owed considerable money due to the turbulent times he had lived through, compelled him to insist he needed no financial assistance from his relatives.

Jean had offered both her sympathies and desire to help.

Do tell her, (he wrote Kate) that I need no financial help. And never would have accepted the same under any circumstances. . . . My letter simply gave description of the terrible ordeal through which I have passed. That is over and occupation will soon follow. Nevertheless, I appreciate her good feeling. And hope she may recover from that injury to her knee . . . and should I meet her in Cal. some day, will have my pockets well filled with yellow toys to meet all emergencies. . . .

One last letter traversed the continent to California.

Pro Principe Jan. 27th 1899

Dear Kate

With the occupation of the Island by the Americans brings brighter prospects and a general revival of business. And if the Cubans are successful in negotiating a loan of $40,000,000 (guaranteed by Cuban House entries) everything will assume a new aspect, and the County become contented.

Their Army has never received one credit and fought simply through patriotism and hatred of the Spaniards, but must have some means of starting again in the world. . . .

Robert probably wrote of that phase of his adopted land's history with more insight than did later historians, for he had been a cog in the machinery of the Revolution. He had survived it.

He never managed the trip to California, nor did he see his beloved kin again. His trials finally ended in Cuba. After his death, however, there were a few more paragraphs to finish the saga of his long adventure. In a letter dated Nov. 8, but with no year furnished, Jean wrote Albert of "Poor Bob's death." It happened at Puerto Prince on October 5, most likely in 1900.

A young man, claiming to be Robert's son, Alberto Bruce, wrote Jean telling her that his father had died after an illness of six months, like a bird going to sleep peacefully. He had, Alberto wrote, three other children by "some woman," and had died in debt. A final tribute was paid to this man who had endured so much suffering. All the people loved him and carried him on their shoulders as the bands played. The company for whom he had worked so long and faithfully paid half the funeral costs, and all Cuba's prominent citizens came to honor him.

Jean doubted the debt part of the story, and with ample reason. Robert had previously returned some gold she had sent him, stating he had all he needed. The return address on his letter was Ferro Carril, the ranch he owned in Puerto Prince.

8 Big Tree Station: The Together Times

May, 1878 to April 17, 1884

These were the together-again times for Azelia and Albert. They both worked at the Big Tree Station complex. Work, school and medical problems had separated them in the first six years of their married life, and they had experienced the misery of losing three babies, but now they enjoyed the beauty and tranquillity of the mountains with incomes for both. Together they earned $80 per month. Albert's wages did not compare to his earnings at the mines, but living conditions and the surroundings far exceeded what he had previously endured.

He worked at everything, wherever he was needed. He improved the efficiency of the water-powered sawmill, did blacksmithing, and built many of the structures for the growing complex. He also beautified the grounds by building a fountain in front of the Hotel.

Azelia's own years of learning and training stepped forward as she sewed linens for the Hotel and entertained its guests by playing the organ.

Miss King was a piano teacher of statewide repute and known to both Azelia and her mother. She decided to widen the range of her activities by visiting YoSemite.

YO SEMITE FALLS HOTEL
(Formerly Hutchings)
John K. Barnard, Proprietor

Connected with this Hotel are
J. C. Smith's Celebrated
Hot and Cold Bathing Establishment,
Post Office, Telegraph Office,
and Wells Fargo's Express.

From YoSemite Valley, on May 31, 1878, and under the above letterhead, Miss M. King wrote her friend Azelia and, in so doing, spoke of the times. It was a stormy day. She hoped that Al was better, was totally delighted with the beautiful view before her as she entered the Valley and was sorry she had not brought her Empress cloth dress, as it would have been useful in the evening. An Earl and his party had arrived on the previous day, and she commented further:

> It seems that Black (another innkeeper) fees the driver to take tourists to his hotel, so that many do not come here, who would otherwise . . . travelers are coming in from Calaveras & I think are being advised that route. . . . I like Mrs. B. very well & the girls, particularly Fanny. I do not see much chance though of making more than the $10. I have been helping to make sheets. The machine was horribly out of order, but was better since being cleaned. The piano is very much out of tune. They (the musicians) are hoping for some tuner to come along. . . .

November, 1878

DISASTER!
Fire swept through the Big Tree complex, ravaging everything except the stables and Long White (a lodging building.) The Washburn-Bruce-Cook triumvirate could have viewed the smoldering heap of ruins as a turning point to complete calamity, but instead immediately began with rebuilding plans, and their sawmill went on full steam.

Albert's varied abilities went on full steam, also, working on the construction of the grand new edifice; he was paid $504 above his wages in appreciation of his dedicated services.

The interior was decorated handsomely by Albert's sisters, Jean and Fannie, as well as Johnny Bridle's wife, Catherine. The Hotel opened on April 1, 1879, only a few months after its predecessor had fallen in flames.

The building was a model of luxury with a wide veranda supported by pillars. Many windows looked out past the stairs to the arriving stages with their guests. Those who graced its bedrooms,

Big Tree Station prior to the November 29, 1878 fire, which destroyed all the buildings except Clark Cottage, on the right. *(Roberta Bruce Phillips Collection.)*

worked at the sawmill along with his father-in-law, William Van Campen. Azelia again sewed linens for the Hotel. The pattern of their life seemed to be settled in its serenity.

But not quite.

November, 1881 ADMINISTRATOR'S SALE!

A meticulous and long inventory was compiled of all the property of Ira Van Campen of the Elkhorn Ranch near Hornitos. His ranch was comprised of 474

dining room and reception rooms were to write of it with words of praise, remembering always their time at Big Tree Station in the Sierra, as well as the gracious hospitality of the Washburns and Johnny Bridle Bruce, the dominant figures in its management.

That same year of 1879 another great event came about. Ten years after their first meeting, Azelia and Albert's fourth child, Albert Henry Bruce was born on July 10. Named after Albert Henry Washburn, he was the couple's first child to survive infancy.

In that year, too, Albert returned to work at the Washington Mine, and there in Hornitos another son, Jay Cook Bruce, entered the world on September 20, 1881. The parents gave careful regard to family when naming their children, the latest being named after another of Albert's brothers-in-law, John Jay Cook.

Then in late 1881, only a few months after the baby's arrival, the Washington Mine was sold and the family returned to Wawona where Albert

After the 1878 fire, Johnny Bridle Bruce and Henry Washburn built this gracious replacement. It stands today as a monument to their vision. Bald Rock dominates the background. *(Mariposa History Center.)*

acres of agricultural land and came with house, fences, barn, a granary and such improvements that had made a working ranch both viable and comfortable. The inventory was careful to include all the possessions this pioneer had accumulated in his 30-year residency. A mower, a seed sower, gang plow and three single plows, three wagons and one stallion, two jacks and two jennies, along with 48 hogs, were just a few of the numerous items to be auctioned. Mares with their sucking colts were slated for sale. This would close an era of a man who had, in 1849, crossed the untamed plains in an oxen-pulled covered wagon and chose this landscape, before California saw statehood, as the site for the rest of his history.

Even his breech-loading rifle would be sold.

Ira had crossed a continent, undergone the hardships of new beginnings in a land so different from his native Allegheny County of New York State, and had persevered as pilgrims must. He certainly would have never prophesied this closure to his life.

It was Brother William who made the revelatory statement to county officials. He had talked with Ira near Merced on the 4th day of September, and his brother had then confessed that he was overcome and beat out by handling his wheat.

William wrote: "I saw that he was laboring under mental difficulties. He talked of putting himself out of the way. I tried to dissuade him from committing anything so rash."

But William's pleading was no match for Ira's terrible and continuing distress. Only five days later, on the night of September 9, 1881, William was awakened by a thud that to him sounded much like the falling of a heavy body, but was, in actuality, the report of Ira's gun from the outhouse as he shot himself in the head.

He was fifty-six. He left no children, but did leave a twenty-five-year-old wife, Nancy, who resided in Owego, New York. It was suspected that Nancy could have been a mail-order bride who went West to Ira, took a look at the territory and turned right around for New York. Perhaps this, as well as the heavy burden of handling his crops, had added to Ira's terrible depression.

Business affairs, and sometimes the personal, did not always progress smoothly. Along the way, something happened. In a letter to her brother, Albert, an aggrieved Fannie wrote of her distress and disenchantment. The primary reason for her bitterness is unknown, but it obviously had to do with the smirching of her son-in-law's name.

Dear Brother Al,

I thank you my brother for your kind words and acts to George as he is my child's husband, but Henry and Johnny I claim no further relationship with for the stain they put on his name of one so nearly connected with J. J. Cook, whose money made them and whom Henry bled so freely to establish himself years ago. I can never forgive them for their trying to put a stain on my family. May God forgive their ingratitude and bless for your brotherly love to me in not joining them in their persecutions of George whom as an Odd Fellows they should have shielded. . . .

Affectionate Sister,
Fannie

Fannie was doubtlessly referring to Henry Washburn, business associate of her husband as well as her brother-in-law, and Johnny Bridle Bruce, her nephew.

On September 10, 1882, a change came to Big Tree Station, and it was one which would be inscribed upon the future. Jean Washburn learned that the Western Mono word for Big Tree was a sound—Wah Woh Nau—a call made by the great horned owl, and she prevailed upon her husband to change the name of Big Tree Station to Wawona.

In 1882 another inventory was taken.

A careful and complete audit of all the property of the Big Tree Hotel complex was compiled. Valuation was listed for every article, from the main hotel building, assessed at $13,500, to a hay press, valued at $100. Listed in this meticulous appraisal were a 16-room Cottage, two stables and a store house. One sawmill was valued at $1,000, with the logs and lumber in the yard at another $1,000. The bedding and furniture in 45 lodging rooms were worth $1,920. A yoke of oxen appraised at $500 was over twice what six cows were worth at $225. There was $1,500 in stock in the store. And on it went, the total value of these assets being $50,070, and the cash on hand $990

The boundaries of the real property were carefully noted and included a sawmill and water ditch, separately evaluated at $4,800.

A tragic reason lay behind this time-consuming inventory and appraisal. Johnny Bridle Bruce had died. He was only forty-four. At the time of his death he owned one-fourth of all the Big Tree holdings, and this now went to his wife, Catherine.

There were no debts nor any claims against his estate.

Also left were three young daughters, Charlotte, Fannie and Alice.

An epic was represented here, beginning with that first rude cottage of Galen Clark, and growing into a favored resort well-known in other parts of the world and by presidents and royalty.

Having lost his affable partner, Henry Washburn was now compelled to lean more on two of his large family of brothers from Putney, Vermont. John Stephen, number 14 of their father's sons, was now forty-four. He had married Ellen M. Taft, but was now a widower. Like his predecessor, Johnny Bridle, John was congenial and sociable, the perfect host for the Hotel. He often met the incoming stage from Raymond, feather duster in hand, to relieve his guests of layers of trail grime. Edward, the other brother to heed Henry's call for help, became secretary and bookkeeper. This duo left Henry free to go out scouting for better roads and better transportation to get there.

At Henry Washburn's home in San Francisco on March 13, 1884, another significant happening occurred. Another child came to Azelia and Albert, and again they bestowed their respect upon Henry when they named their daughter Henrietta Patty.

With their family growing, the couple finally began putting their dreams into action when they filed a homestead claim for 160 acres in the Wawona area.

The Homestead Law of 1862, under which Albert filed his claim, held that any citizen willing to go through the process of proving a claim would be given title.

Part of the requirement was the building of a house, to be lived in, plus a fee of $200.

Henry Washburn viewed Albert's filing with deep suspicion and distrust, and fearing that the talented and energetic couple would build a competitive hotel, he fired not only both of them, but Azelia's father, William Van Campen. He was resolute in his determination that no competition confront him, telling Albert that no lumber would be sold him, as it was all needed for his own building purposes. Apparently, family ties were strung along the lower border of this tapestry of events. A bad time lay ahead for Azelia and Albert.

There was little weaponry in their arsenal to fight back, but Albert and Azelia used one retaliatory tool they did possess. So watch out, Henry! They promptly renamed their daughter, Harriet Howard. She would henceforth be known as Hattie. Albert Henry kept his name.

But all was far from lost, as Azelia had a wily father. With presentiments of Washburn's future actions, William Van Campen took away all the slabs and wasted material from the Washburn sawmill and relocated them onto the homestead property. He then began to build the pre-emption house, one of the requirements to qualify for claiming the land.

Albert was desperate for money, not only to support his family, but to pay the $200 homestead fee. He headed for Mariposa on foot to check out the mines between there and Hornitos, finally finding work at the Quartz Mountain Mine.

When Henry Washburn learned that Azelia's father was building a house for those he considered his adversaries, he flew into some action of his own by ordering the family to vacate the old boarding house in which they had been living. He had not counted on Azelia's stiff resolution. She flatly refused to leave until her own house was completed.

William Van Campen finished Azelia's house, filled a lean-to with stove wood and then headed to his own homestead in the Sandy Mush area of Merced County.

Land was becoming more scarce in direct proportion to the demand. On April 14, 1884, Albert filed for his second homestead. The property contained two choice attractions already popular with tourists. One was the Fern Grotto, a sort of perpendicular cavern bordered with immense and varied shaped boulders. It was shady and luxuriously green with ferns. A stream flowed through it to give moisture to the growth of the ferns. The second scenic wonder was Chilnualna Falls, also boulder-encased and flowing in a series of falls.

Henry Washburn had built a small cabin near the falls. A platform extending from it served as the stage stop for his guests who visited the falls. His rift with Azelia and Albert had begun to heal when he realized the couple had no intention to compete. He then signed over his claim to the cabin:

This is to certify that we have this day sold to

Albert Bruce for one dollar in hand paid,
A certain house or cabin situated on margin
of Chilnualna Creek releasing all right and
title to said house or cabin.

July 29, 1884,
Signed Washburn & Co.

Though she persevered with her boarders, gave piano lessons and sewed diligently for the ladies, Harriet Van Campen had long complained of pain. She was relieved of all her suffering when she passed away on September 9, 1884. She left her Merced home to her son, Barnes.

The doctor who had attended Harriet promptly sued Barnes for unpaid bills. On the opposite side of this action, Azelia claimed her mother had been improperly medicated with too-strong prescriptions, and in a letter of October 1, 1884, she wrote her husband of her anxiety about Barnes' lawsuit:

Stay with him through this and aid him all possible. Let me know what lawyer he will have and all that is interesting concerning the affair as soon as practical, but of course, be careful not to write any you would not want seen as this office is not conducted on strict principles. . . .

Clearly, Azelia still chafed about their earlier treatment, for it was the Washburns who ran the local post office. She went on to advise Albert:

I hear that Henry is at Merced. Suppose he had to be on hand to urge you to homestead or something else he got in his head but don't you be a daub of clay in any molder's hand.

Her distraction continued with her opinion of her mother's doctor when she wrote:

. . . I regret from the bottom of my heart that she even had him and shall always feel strange about it. She mentioned again that she felt the medicine he had prescribed was too strong.

Winter closed in, and it was a mean one. The slab cabin grew colder. Azelia gathered all the materials she could find to stuff into the holes and cracks of their rudimentary preemption house, and as she stood on a table to chink the higher cracks, the children, Bertie (Albert Henry) and

Jay, worked on those close to the floor. Winds swept in snow through the cracks, covering them in their beds. Three times each week, Azelia wrapped her feet in barley sacks and made her laborious way down to the post office to drop off or pick up her mail.

At this time, Barnes owned his own blacksmith shop, "The Celebrated Milburn Wagon" at Plainsburg, where he not only worked as a blacksmith, but constructed wagons. He implored his sister not to worry about him, as he knew he would

Aziel Barnes Van Campen was a carpenter, a blacksmith, and a well-known wagon maker. In his seventies, gifted with a remarkable memory, he had the vision to set down his recollections of an earlier time. *(Roberta Bruce Phillips Collection.)*

pull through somehow and come out on top of the heap yet. He was terribly lonesome and dreaded the coming winter. Already the wind and rain forced him "to stay in this old shop."

Later, Barnes took time from his blacksmithing to help their father with the homestead house, and years down the road he wrote in a lengthy memoir how much pleasure this had afforded him. He, too, homesteaded at Wawona, but in 1904 sold his 160 acres to Edward Washburn for $10 per acre.

Barnes was well-known for his whistle. Apparently a happy man and decidedly a man devoted to God, he continually whistled throughout his working days. But then he married Ella Hosser, a girl from Ohio, and when later he learned she was unable to produce heirs, Barnes never again pursed his lips to whistle.

The times were lean for many. In the fall of 1894, Albert's friend, H. A. Hanson, wrote him from Sacramento. "Just doing so so ascending to the hard times. Driving carriage from 12 in the day to 12 at night and sometimes all night." The job had to be miserable, for the nights were cold and frosty, and he became ill for 18 days, not able to open his mouth for six of those 18. Interestingly, he and his wife expected to go to the Valley to work in the spring, and to him Wawona was still "the Station."

Albert was a determined survivor; the times demanded it. Just before the Christmas of 1884, he wrote his dear Azelia from Quartz Mountain Mine where he was working. Like his friend, Hanson, he was working from daylight to dark and suffering miserably. However, such misery did not preclude him from protecting his interests "The gentleman that was up there is one of the heaviest stockholders in this Comp. came to see me. Was very discouraged. People on the route told him he was throwing money away. I took him in the mine. Lied to him like a trooper, until I drove away the blues. When he got back to Hotel he would not take $3.00 per share for stock that he was ready to sacrifice and all through a little cheek of mine assumed for the occasion. He said he hoped I would make a success of the mine and he would remember me liberally."

Albert did enjoy optimism, even as he suffered from the poor conditions of his life away from his home hearth. "Mose has promised to help me in affairs up there after everything is in operation here. Asked me to stick to him and he would stick to me. I believe he will make about $35,000 from this venture. We have been unable to do much on account of rain the past week. I am in rags with no place to sleep. Am forcing myself on Geo. Chittendens. We occupy the same bed in a damp cold shanty."

And then, as in the days at Belmont and Bodie, he admonished his wife to save every dollar that she could. He was working for the purpose of caring for his family and expected that things would be better by summer.

But summer was months away.

At the Wawona homestead, Azelia was practically isolated. Few white residents braved wintering there, and with the tourists gone, the Hotel had long since closed for the season. By Christmas the situation had gone from lean to leaner. Albert was 80 miles away, still at Quartz Mountain. The meat supply had been exhausted months earlier, and without guns there seemed no hope to re-supply the larder.

The time was considerably brightened for the children when a parcel of toys arrived from Albert. The following day two packages of toys arrived, one from their Aunt Jean and the other from Fannie Cook, also an aunt.

On the eastern base of Chowchilla Mountain, a few other all-year residents of the area lived. They were a handful of Chowchilla Indians, among them the camp's shaman, Bullock, and his woman, Susie; her sister, Short and Dirty; Bullock's daughter, Mary Ann, and her man, Bushhead Tom. Two orphans, Joe and Josey Amos, also lived in the camp. They usually kept to themselves.

It was from this quarter that the best and least expected gift arrived on the morning of Christmas Eve when Azelia answered a knock on the door of her slab house. There stood Mary Ann and Joe. When Azelia invited them in, she was presented with a hunk of venison. "Tom, he shoot deer," Mary Ann told an amazed Azelia, at the same time holding up two fingers. Then she explained her gift. "Indians think maybe you no got meat for Christmas dinner." Once Azelia had recovered from her surprise, she brewed coffee and sliced fresh baked bread and invited the two, who were warming their feet by the stove, for a repast. They visited for a time, and when Mary Ann and Joe were ready to leave, Azelia slipped a silver dollar into the woman's hand and said, "You tell Tom to buy some more cartridges for his gun. Then, when you have plenty of venison, bring us some and I will pay you more." She then wrapped a loaf of bread and gave it to her benefactor, saying, "Take this for your dinner tomorrow." For the remainder of that winter there was no shortage of meat.

From this encounter a special friendship grew between the two women. For the next several years, Mary Ann was a weekly visitor in the Bruce home. Azelia taught her new friend how to make bread and prepare sage dressing to stuff venison. And Joe taught the boys about tracking and hunting game, which in coming years would greatly benefit Jay.

In March of 1885, Albert went to San Francisco to buy machinery for the company. He made $50 commission from the houses through which he had traded and sent $40 to Azelia to get things for the house.

He did more than that while in the City. He called on Glory Hallelujah Miller, a Spiritualist, and gave his wife a detailed account of that visit.

> Your Mother came to me and begged forgiveness for her harsh thoughtless treatment of me. Said she believed me foolish while in the body, but now knew me to be one of nature's noblemen and of all persons best suited to you for a husband. Said if she had understood me could not help but love me, that these were hard confessions to make, but came to do me justice. That I was your Saviour and that she was glad to come back and make reconciliations from the other side. That her progression and yours and Barnes depended on me. In fact, spoke kindly and beautiful such praises of myself I never expected from her lips

either on this or the other side of life . . . said that we had taken the right steps in the land question and would succeed beyond our expectation, would have a fine home and plenty . . . and that Barnes would not lose the Merced property to the doctor who had long wanted it. . . . Now mind you, during all this conversation your Mother's identity was as perfect as if she was there in physical body.

Albert ended the letter by saying he sent books for Bert and Jay. "Tell Bertie he must be able to read when I come up."

Plans for the homestead house were in the works. Albert insisted on a fine home that would make them proud, and he continued working at the mines to finance it while Azelia did the designing. Its location was close to the Grotto[1] so they would be able to stop tourists from taking the ferns.

William Van Campen began clearing the land for his daughter's house. He worked with a team of horses and seemed to outlast them in his will to finish the house. On April 24, 1885, Azelia wrote to a still absent husband that "Father has been working on the house, but has only foundation laid so far. Although he has worked very hard has had no help whatever and has made a horse of himself to haul and pull immense timbers. . . . John and Stella[2] were married on 22nd of April. We had invitations, came the day after the wedding. Jean was in for teeth and toe nail."

She mentioned visiting the falls, which were lovely. Fannie had written a very pretty poem on the falls and the Grotto. Her father was busy, she went on to tell Albert, not only with their new house, but he had to see about a timber claim as well as a half-section of school land to which he was entitled. He wanted to see about Section 16, which would be near the big bridge.

---

1. Today the Grotto is almost barren. A road runs within 20 feet of it and few ferns grow there now.
2. Innkeeper John Washburn married Estella Hill, the daughter of resident landscape artist Thomas Hill, who maintained his studio only a few feet below the Hotel.

9 The Homestead

There was no doubt Aziel Barnes Van Campen was brother to Azelia, cut from the same metal of steely industriousness and fortitude. In 1866, at eighteen, he apprenticed himself to a carpenter, but the "here today and somewhere else tomorrow" aspect of the job did not suit him, so said he in a lengthy memoir that he later presented to Dr. Carl P. Russell and Ernest P. Leavitt, Yosemite National Park officials.

In that same year of 1866, he acquired a house and lot for $125 on the corner of 6th and Bullion in Mariposa, only to lose it in the town's disastrous fire.

Disasters seemed to seek out Barnes. At high noon (he remembered it well!) on Friday, August 16, 1878, his house burned, and with it 16 years of work lost forever. This was the fourth fire he suffered in 18 years of labor.

Aziel Barnes Van Campen built this still-standing house on Chilnualna Road. Certainly not as grand as the Parthenon, but with a layer of history that spells part of Wawona's past.

Although he had not wished to use his carpenter training for a career, it held him in good stead throughout his life. He built several houses in Wawona, one the shingle-roofed Catherine Leitch house on Chilnualna Drive, and surviving still as a sturdy reminder of that pioneering age. He also built himself a house on his homesteaded property. It was a fine home, rustic-sided and graced with beautiful scrolls on all the posts. It boasted three bedrooms, a large parlor and living room and a kitchen with a pantry to one side. Inside, solid mahogany furniture with black horsehair upholstery filled the rooms.

For ten months he worked on Azelia and Albert's homestead house, and the labor afforded him a special joy, he was always eager to say.

After his return to his shop in Plainsburg, he wrote his sister that : "I let Father have a wagon to bring up to use up there and if I never call for it, it is yours and yours alone. If I sell out, I will probably give it to you."

Whatever Azelia next wrote Albert set him on the defensive, and he offered a hasty reply on May 24, 1885. He was still working at Quartz Mountain.

From the tone of your last you seem to think I am enjoying every luxury, neglecting family & etc. all for my own especial benefit. I can forgive all this knowing as I well do your state of mind and temperament. But let me tell you once and for all that I am making every sacrifice of myself doing so freely and with good heart to benefit you and the little ones. I have started to establish a home for you and if God spares my life and health will leave you well fixed when I shove off this mortal coil (perhaps for some old one-eyed rancher to enjoy the fruits of my labor.) You seem to think I am not earning much here, again you mistake, I am doing better than for years. Have about $200 in cash beside clearing off old debts.

It was natural that Azelia missed Albert with a terrible longing. She was raising three children alone, still existing in a rustic cabin, and among relatives who were not all as friendly as they once had been toward her. It was natural, too, that she beseeched him to come home. But it really got his back up. He fired off another letter at once.

I know exactly what I am doing. And when you learn to have proper faith in the only one living who has or would stick to you, you will be wise. And when you would have me throw up $4.00 per day to come up there and be dogged about for $25 per month. Besides being the recipient of back-handed insult. You forget that I am a Bruce. That blood flows through my veins from a line of ancestry that knew no such word as fail. No matter what you may think, I am working for an object. That object I will obtain, though to reach it I leave a trail of sweat and blood. I hope you will abandon the idea that I am living luxuriously and having everything my heart desires and money can furnish. Poor me that am destitute of even a pair of overhands or clothing for my feet, except what I pick up.

Once Albert had defended himself, he went on to other matters. But whatever Azelia's words had been, Albert was still stung and let her know so, even while discussing the homestead house.

I object to shake house. It is labor thrown away. I again say have lumber got at Thurman's and bill sent to me. Or I will ship the cash when you deign to send me word. I do not want anything there unless fit to live in and be comfortable. It is just as easy to do things right now as at some future time. I will pay for the land myself and long as you have bank account. . . . Now attend to this house business and let the timber your Father has cut be used for other buildings. Make a plan for a good-sized, decent looking shanty. I may have money enough to build in style before you are aware that I am doing anything. So mind what I say for once in your life.

Albert's injured feelings had mended by July 10, 1885, when he again wrote Azelia, this time strictly a matter of business. He was in Mariposa. "I am here after a tiresome ride. Got here worn out so I could hardly walk." He had gone to the court house, apparently to claim on the land.

The Homestead cannot be taken up as we wish. Each one quarter has to join the other without separation so choose your location to best advantage possible, and send me a diagram marked as you wish. The expense of pre-emption will be $220, advertising and all. . . . Be careful in choosing the next one-quarter section to get Grotto in and good land. I have in my pocket $320 gold coin and with what is due me

at the mine will have somewhere about $400 to deposit. . . .

Mines played out. Their rich promise too often left the stockholders at an altar bereft of dividends and their employees bereft of wages. Albert moved to the Eureka Mine, outside Mariposa to the East, but by August 10, 1885, when he again wrote to Azelia, that mine had also laid off most of the workers. In fact, Albert was the only employee still on the payroll. He wrote: "How long the job will last is hard telling. All the Rhode Island companies have made decided failures in everything handled here commencing with Old Houghton to Eureka Company." And he feared he might not get up to Wawona before proving up on the homestead.

Trouble sought out Barnes again. "I expect you know he has been burned out again saving only one wagon and the clothes he had on. Expect he was at church praying for you while his shop was burning." It was a cryptic note from Albert, who knew well Barnes prayed twice daily for all those he considered strayed sheep from the flock of the Lord, as well as for himself and his "wicked ways."

Interest and optimism once more cheered Albert. The superintendent of the Quartz Mountain Mine, Mr. Chodzko, bought the Frances Ledge and asked Albert to go there to put up a ten-stamp mill at a salary of $5 per day. Additionally, "Parties from Providence" (probably the stockholders) arrived on the scene, and Albert felt he had "full opportunity of having full charge of everything with the hope of making a grand success. I told the party if the Company would furnish $10,000 I would guarantee to bring things to a successful issue. . . . If I can get them to run the mine for six months I will feather my nest beside making a reputation."

He still hoped for his own mine. ". . . If I stay here, will have chance to open up a vein of my own from which I got $125 per ton assay from Cropping and will be able to work my rock here . . . now is the time to secure mining property. I could have made bushels of coin if I had got Buena Vista and Frances."

It was August and time to plan for a winter that Azelia would soon confront. "I think we had better lay in a bill of goods for the winter. I will either send or go below for them any time the old man will have them. So make out your list and get enough of everything to have comfort through winter."

At last Albert returned to Wawona. In September, he and Azelia's father took up the supplies he had suggested she order and stocked up on firewood. But by January it was back to the mines and Azelia was again left without a husband. Her comfort in a grand house was closer than ever before, though.

Albert's faithful letters kept his wife apprised always of his whereabouts, intentions and hopes. He also directed her as to how she should manage. From Grub Gulch, on April 1, 1886, he wrote:

> Had a stormy ride down, found Mr. Gillette in good humor. Am to start at work in the morning. My first job is putting up engine and boiler and five extra stamps in mill. Hardly think my job will be to run donkey hoisting work. . . . I have taken board at Anderson's Hotel at $6 per week less than I thought to pay. . . . Write Barnes, have price of doors and windows you want. . . .

Grub Gulch saw him only a short time. In June of that same year, he returned home with six-months pay in his pocket and a woman to help Azelia.

Both family and prospects were on the ascendancy. On July 3, 1886, Azelia and Albert welcomed another daughter when Jeanie Frances joined their ranks. Although she had just missed being born on that grandest of days, the Fourth of July, she came into the world a special child. She was the first Bruce child to be born in Wawona, and she had the gift.

Since the midwife was late on the scene, Albert attended her birth. Jean Washburn sent her personal maid, Lady Jackson, over from the Hotel to care for Azelia and the children.

In November, the homestead house, designed by Azelia and built by her brother and father, was

The Homestead House, 1889. On the porch, left to right, are Jay, William, Azelia, Jeanie, Albert Henry, Albert O., and Harriet. Albert O. proudly shows his Ownership Certificate. *(Mariposa County History Center.)*

completed. It was as grand as the pre-emption house was simple, and was undoubtedly the grandest home in Wawona, product of Albert's insistence for the best and Azelia's meticulous planning. It boasted a parlor with wall-to-wall carpeting and a grand piano. A large dining room housed an organ in the corner and a long table in the middle where the family could gather for meals, learning and lively discussion, the latter always fierce and competitive. A glassed-in conservatory stretched along one side to showcase an assortment of plants. Books on every subject from medicine to political philosophy and from carpentry to science filled the library. At the rear of the house a large kitchen and pantry were located.

And how did Azelia acquire the grand piano? Why, it was brought across the plains from the East, hauled by a pair of oxen, its four heavy legs sticking up toward the sky! This was the story passed down by Bill and Bert Bruce, the family comedians. In actuality, Albert bought it for his wife from Judge Grant when the Judge Grant Hotel closed down. Though its legs might have still been pointing upward, the piano had a few less miles to travel, the hotel being located between the William Sell Bridge and Worman Road on today's Highway 49.

Albert also bought a lot of glassware, including stemmed goblets in blue, red, green and brown and white finger bowls and whiskey glasses just large enough to hold one tablespoon of liquor.

A day of momentous note came to pass.

Given under my hand, at the City of Washington, the seventh day of March, in the year of our Lord, one thousand eight hundred and ninety-two, and of the Independence of the United States the one hundred and sixteenth, By the President, Benjamin Harrison.

Thus the Homestead, located in Section 35 of Wawona and belonging to Azelia and Albert Bruce, was secure. The paper had been signed by the president.

The Homestead House was a showplace in its time. A library and an arboretum helped grace the interior. The house burned in the 1950s. *(Roberta Bruce Phillips Collection.)*

With their ownership irrevocably established, a recent survey of Yosemite Park showing the North line of their property being the South line of the park, Albert and Azelia were at last able to shed their anxieties. With the election of Benjamin Harrison as president, festivities seemed to be in order. So Albert came home happy, with a couple of

drinks under his belt. The long table was set for supper when he, happy visions of homestead security dancing in his head, arrived home. His joy brimming, he bumped against the table, knocking food and dishes to the floor. This caused so much turmoil in the household that the kids were sent to bed without their supper!

"Mother and Father blessed the Republican party and hoped they would always remain in office," daughter Hattie wrote in a long memoir to John C. Preston, then superintendent of Yosemite National Park, in 1956.

Their former antagonists, the Washburns, finding the family determined to stay on their land and likely judging they offered no competition, decided they made better allies than adversaries. Azelia and Albert were asked to work for the hotel complex. Albert did everything. He worked at a variety of positions, including store clerk and saloon keeper, handyman and carpenter, as well as foreman for the sawmill. Azelia worked far into the night on a treadle sewing machine, sewing linens for the Hotel. They worked for the Wawona Hotel Company from that time until they retired.

They planted wheat and hay on their land, fenced and cross fenced the property in accordance with the Homestead Act, and canned all they could from the garden to make it through the winter. Azelia's father continued his tremendous help, plowing and fencing, helping with the hay harvest. Azelia worked alongside, helping with the felling of trees and carrying armfuls of brush to pile on top the fences to outsmart the foraging deer.

The Fern Grotto and Chilnualna Falls, second only to the Mariposa Grove of Big Trees in tourist

The sign on Wawona's General Store summed up its functions. Albert Olcott Bruce worked here from the late 1800s to the early 1900s.

with grain, and Azelia kept a luxurious sheaf of it, tied with a broad, white ribbon, in the corner of her parlor, both pride and proof that their land had been proved upon.

Much of Wawona's history was marked by triumphs and tragedies. On August 27, 1887, another tragedy struck at the heart of the family. Johnny Bridle's widow, Catherine, died. She was only thirty-five. Jean and Henry Washburn quickly committed to the raising of their three little grandnieces, bestowing upon them through their growing-up years the same privileges enjoyed by their daughter, Jeanie.

As a resort, Wawona closed down in the winter, and as a community, it took on another life. It was a life relentlessly struggling for survival by the few residents

attractions, was a must for so many of the Wawona Hotel guests. One day a group of tourists from Scotland passed the homestead on their way to view the falls and on their way passed Barnes and the whole family in the field raking hay. One of the group couldn't resist relating his impressions later to Albert, who was working at the Hotel store. "I saw what I never thought I would see in America. A brute of a *mon* out in the hot sun, and his bonny wife raking hay same as in Russia, and their four beautiful children asleep in the hay stack."

Never a farmer by nature, choice or attitude, Albert was humiliated and never acknowledged that the family was his own.

What might have equally amazed the tourist was another scene, though he never witnessed it. Azelia was on her way home, little children alongside, a baby in its blue buggy and another on the way. Sharing space in the buggy with the baby was a heavy sack of potatoes. Disaster struck. The springs of the carriage broke. There was nothing else to do but lift the baby out of the buggy and, with the other youngsters in tow, trudge home. Azelia then had to make trip after trip to the collapsed carriage for the potatoes.

The wheat grew six feet tall, with heads heavy

who stayed there year round. With the constant work of keeping roads cleared of snow and roofs cleared of snow, it can't be said that life slowed or the spirit eased; they merely took on another tone. When heavy snow clogged the roads the stages stopped. The Hotel closed and the Washburns went to San Francisco for the winter.

The severe winter of 1888–89 was not likely to be forgotten by anyone who had been tested by it or lived through it. Heavy snows piled up to six feet on the roads. When the hay in the Bruce barn ran out, it took a family member from four o'clock in the bitter morning until ten o'clock at night to drive their horses to Washburn's barn, less than two miles away.

On the opposite side of the river, the Washburn sawmill collapsed from the snow.

That winter would likely be remembered for another reason. On October 8, 1888, an event of great note occurred. The first son to be born in Chilnualna Park, the homestead, came into the world. He was William Wallace Bruce, most likely named after his Grandfather Van Campen, and possibly after the compatriot of Robert of Bruce, William Wallace, an early Scots fighting hero.

Azelia's three snappily dressed little angels: Harriet, Jeanette, and Jay Bruce, about 1888.
(Roberta Bruce Phillips Collection.)

With Azelia and Albert now permanently settled in their homestead house, few letters between the two now exist, and so their history meshes with that of Wawona's history and their children's.

On December 20, 1890, William Van Campen wrote his will, leaving his ranch in the Sandy Mush area to Azelia. Once all his debts were paid, she was to have both it and all the cattle and stock. The will was witnessed by A. Pleasaccia of Merced and drawn up by John L. Cameraro.

November, 1892.

Azelia cared for her father on the homestead in his last days. She was feeding him some custard when he chided her for not filling and cleaning the lamps. "Father, I did it this morning," she told him. He replied, "Azelia, the lights grow dim." And with that he died, the spoon still in his mouth.

Gus Wintermute built William's coffin, which was put in the parlor. Azelia covered it with black felt and lined it with white satin. The 23rd Psalm

Built to satisfy the tourists' increasing demands for comfort, the Stoneman House enjoyed a short life. Perhaps only the fire that destroyed it in 1896 could cure the many ills that plagued it.
(Yosemite National Park Collection.)

was read at his funeral, after which he was buried on the homestead property. A fence designated the spot until 1924, but no marker further identified his resting place. The story goes that the coffin was dug up by a back hoe during excavation for the foundation of a house. At that time, no one could say for sure to whom it belonged and it was quickly covered up as the construction continued, with the implication that William still lies there in a field he once tended.

The Sentinel Hotel, located on the bank of the Merced River in Yosemite Valley's Old Village, was marked with charm and graciousness. A. B. Glasscock, who named it, ran the hotel from 1894 until his death in 1897. At that time Jay Bruce Cook took over its operation. *(Mariposa History Center Collection.)*

Albert wanted to expand his field of operation. He began seriously thinking of opening a store and saloon in Yosemite Valley. He reasoned the burgeoning numbers of tourists would be sure to use such an establishment. So he sought the advice of John Jay Cook, who had been successful in his own investments. That man's answer was succinct. "My opinion is that you could not make 50 cents a day on the year's average with store & saloon in Yosemite after paying expenses of store & saloon and that your troubles would be tenfold what it is now."

Cook was then off to Lake Tahoe, an area he apparently figured more amenable to new enterprise, as he wanted to look at a hotel there.

Albert heeded his advice. He stayed in Wawona.

But John Jay Cook could not content himself with his Wawona interests. Both he and Henry Washburn were respected forces in Yosemite Valley. John Jay was managing Black's Hotel in the Valley in 1880, moving to the management of the Stoneman House in 1888, where he trained his son, Jay Bruce Cook, in the art of running hotels which would satisfy the growing demands of tourists. Jay Bruce Cook was later awarded the lease on the Sentinel Hotel after the death of A. B. Glasscock in 1897.

John Jay Cook's grandson, Ed Baxter, at one time Guardian of the Big Trees and later a State Legislator, was helpful in acquiring the required leases for some of the Cook and Washburn hotel operations in Yosemite Valley.

Azelia's versatility matched that of her husband. She was an artist who painted lovely landscapes, a musician, a seamstress, a teacher, a homemaker and a mother. And if she could be called more of one than the other the mother part would surely head the list.

She began teaching her children the basics of reading, writing and music. Music was an integral part of life in the Bruce household, and Azelia was certainly qualified to teach. She had sung with the San Francisco Opera before her marriage and had been a star pupil on the piano of both her mother, who taught piano in Merced and Hornitos, and of Mrs. King, known for her musical artistry throughout the state.

Impressing upon her children the life-enriching value of musical enjoyment, Azelia encouraged all

Camp A. E. Wood, located at the site of the present Wawona campground, was the seasonal home of the U. S. Cavalry from 1891 to 1906. There is no doubt its presence caused a stir in Wawona life and attitudes. *(Pat Wildt Collection.)*

her sons to play some musical instrument. And they did. The fiddle, mandolin, guitar, piano and organ—they were played by the Bruce boys at any opportunity afforded them. Weddings, dances at the Hotel, any social event calling for some musical interlude all lured these gifted young men to the scene. Nathan "Pike" Phillips, an early guide in the area, was himself enchanted by the chords and taught both Bert and Jay some fiddle hoedowns.

In the evenings, Azelia sat at her organ, accompanying herself by singing operatic arias, her children her awed audience. One evening as she was playing, Gyp, the old bird dog, began to growl, and Azelia, investigating, found three tourists sitting on her porch. The three had taken a moonlight hike to Chilnualna Falls and, hearing her voice, had stood outside to listen for so long that they had finally tired and decided to rest on her porch. "Why do you hide such a marvelous voice?" one of them queried. Azelia's answer was immediate and from the heart. "So as to raise my children away from a big city with only the grandeur of nature around them. Here we are independent and peaceful, free from temptation. We live with God."

In 1891, two arrivals heralded a great change in the Bruce household. One was small, the other rather monumental.

The Wawona Tunnel Tree offered its imposing size and unusual corridor to the four Wawona horseback riders. Pictured are: Jeanie (Jeanette) Bruce; Allen Kilgour, a Cavalryman; Harriet Bruce; and Amos Kinzer, a Cavalryman stationed at Wawona.
(Roberta Bruce Phillips Collection.)

when Congress ceded Yosemite Valley and the Mariposa Grove of Big Trees to the state of California in 1864.

As providential as was the Act ceding Yosemite Valley to the state, no tool of enforcement existed. Sheepherders and cattlemen still brought in their flocks and herds to compact the ground and overgraze the vegetation. Then on October 1, 1890, Yosemite National Park was established, and that same month, looking to Yellowstone Park for precedent, the Secretary of the Interior asked that Army troops be made available as they had been in Yellowstone to look after and protect the park. They would send out scouting parties to "prevent timber cutting, sheep herding, trespassing or spoliation in particular."

On April 6, 1891, Troop I, Fourth Cavalry, stationed at the Presidio, was chosen for duty in the newly-designated national park. Not only was Captain Wood in charge, he was subsequently designated Acting Superintendent of the park. Headquarters for their summer months' duty was established near the site of today's campground. From this camp, mounted patrols went out in search of the errant, who were scattered and many.

The job had its problems. Captain Wood had purchased a map of the area in San Francisco, but it failed the accuracy test. Many patented lands lay within the perimeter of their authority, and roads and trails were few. Within the law which carried no penalties for trespass and within this tract of unclear boundaries, Captain Wood had to invent his own method of operation. He was first an Army man, who from necessity and certainly an innate wisdom, became a mountain man. He took his duties by the teeth, tackling them with a sense of fairness and perception. He studied any available maps, not all of them accurate, sent his troops to scout and assess, and in an amazingly short time had grasped the situation that surrounded him. Still, enforcement was more a theory than reality.

Captain Wood wrote long, explanatory reports to the Secretary of the Interior, in which he mentioned everything from his own actions to the topography of the range. In his report of August 31, 1891, he wrote:

> The lands within the boundaries of this park have been used as a grazing ground by the cattle and sheep owners for many years, and in

On May 17, Troop I of the Fourth Cavalry from the Presidio of San Francisco encamped near Wawona. They had marched the entire 250 miles to reach their destination.

On November 17, the Bruces numbered one more, with the arrival of Edward Washburn Bruce. He was named after Edward Washburn, that rift having been long healed.

The arrival of Troop I with Captain A. E. Wood in charge was no matter of either insignificant or impetuous decision-making, however much it was regarded by sheepherders and ranchers as government intervention. Clearly enough, there had been past government intrusion, though necessary, order to begin what in this country is called a "square deal" with them I wrote a letter to every stock owner whose name and address I could learn in middle and southern California, notifying them that it was my duty to keep all stock off this reservation, and asking them as law-abiding citizens to use due diligence towards keeping their stock away, thereby aiding me in the execution of the will of Congress.

Captain Wood felt that most of the cattle owners, many from the San Joaquin and the coast, generally tried to comply, but many small holders were too poor to hire herders, and their stock drifted up the canyons into the higher mountains when the foothill grazing became sparse.

By the end of May that year, 50,000 sheep began their annual migration from the dried grass of the foothills to the better grazing grounds of the Sierra, and were poised to cross at both the southern and western boundaries of the park. They were divided into bands of from 2,000 to 3,000, with about three herders each and dogs and pack animals to carry supplies. The herders were mostly Portuguese, with a few Chilians, French and Mexicans. Captain Wood was on top of the situation. He wrote:

> They have carried things with a high hand and have 'bulldozed' the poor squatters among these mountains for years. It was no unusual thing for the herder to open the fence and let his sheep into the squatter's small field, where they would eat up everything. . . . I knew that any measure which I might adopt that would rid the mountains of these vandals would be popular, for they are hated by the inhabitants of these regions with a hatred that surpasses belief.

Captain Wood's ideas were quickly formulated, as evidenced in his report to his superior, the Secretary of the Interior. He wrote:

> . . . I knew that there was no penalty attached to a trespass upon this Park, but I also knew that the sheep men were not aware of this, or if they had any ideas upon the subject at all they were very vague and undefined and that decided action upon my part would settle the

question in a very few days, and before they could recover from their surprise I would be master of the situation.

With the law then so nearly impossible to enforce, Cavalry officers in time devised their own unique systems. They began expelling the herders or cattlemen from one end of the park while the sheep or cattle were driven out the opposite side, so often down dangerously steep canyons. Many sheep fell victim to predators or were scattered and lost in the deep canyons. If a man lost his wealth in this manner he wasn't likely to return. Good reasoning? Only until such time as an aggrieved and determined herder planned his own cunning method to defeat the law of the Cavalry. On at least one occasion, a wily herder sent some of his men and pack animals to the other side of the mountain where his sheep would exit if located by the troops. They were found and expelled and, of course, ate the land bare along the passage of their expulsion. The waiting herder then escorted the sheep to other ranges within the park.

Homesteaders within the protected area were allowed to keep their animals on their property on condition it be fenced. Many failed to fence adequately enough to contain the animals, which then grazed park lands.

There were also many mining claims still existing within the park boundaries. Captain Wood gave the miners fair appraisal in his report of September 1, 1892, to the Secretary of the Interior when he wrote:

> Hope is the miners' main stay of life. A miner without hope would be as great a natural curiosity as the Yosemite Valley.

He could have been describing Albert Olcott Bruce!

An astute Captain Wood saw as a necessity a railroad established near the park to facilitate transportation into the area. He then advised that the government buy as many of the patented plots as possible before this should happen, as prices would jump considerably after that time.

10 School Days

The White House graced Wawona's landscape.

In May 1891, Mariposa County officials established the Wawona School district. The following year Albert was appointed a School Board Trustee. Azelia then proceeded to build a school on the southwest corner of the homestead property, on today's Chilnualna Road. It was constructed of white boards, many windows and a front porch. But the children never came. At that time, most of Wawona's school-age children lived on the other side of the river. To access the school they would have to pass by the Cavalry troops, the troop horses and the troops' activities and the parents considered such passing-by as unacceptable.

Their fear could have a legitimate basis. It was said that some of the troops chased the Indian girls. To avoid being raped, the terrified girls would insert sand into their bodies.

A school was subsequently built in the Hotel complex and a later one erected downhill from the Hotel by the Washburns. School opened in April or May, closing in October or November, as suscepti-

The White House, built by Azelia Bruce, saw diners rather than the school children for whom it was intended. Today's school is located on the same site. *(Roberta Bruce Phillips Collection.)*

ble to the weather as the farmers' crops. In the late 1800s and early 1900s, there were few families resident year round and school enrollment was, at best, sketchy. If enrollment dropped too low, school did not keep that season. One year of especially low head count, a dedicated teacher adopted two children to prevent the school closing. A letter to Azelia, dated November 14, 1901, bore out this presumption. Miss Myrtle Scott of Mariposa was seeking the position of schoolteacher at Wawona.

> I know that your school is very small and came near going below the average required this year, so if it would be any help in keeping the school up, I have three little brothers that I could bring up to attend school.
>
> I should have written to your husband hearing that he is clerk, but they told me that you transacted all school affairs for him, and advised me to write to you. I would like very much to teach your school and should I be successful in getting it I would try my best to give satisfaction.

After offering three little brothers as pupils, it probably was hardly necessary to state her keen desire for the position.

Gertrude Hutchings, daughter of James Hutchings, early homesteader and Valley innkeeper, was the first teacher in 1891.

"The White House," a sobriquet fittingly attached to it, enjoyed many other purposes. When A. W. Spelt started his summer camp, Camp Chilnualna, the house intended as a school had its largest room converted into a restaurant.

Its function did not diminish. Jay Bruce, with his family, called it home; others, who with their families enjoyed it as living quarters were A. W. Spelt, Al Bruce, Alice and Tat Ashworth, Nellie and Russell Graham. Hardman used it as a market to sell his vegetables. But its most colorful and perhaps most active time was the era when Jay Robb used it as a speak-easy, selling his bootlegged liquor from there.

The White House never saw benches, blackboard or little children learning to spell and count, but if schools could beget schools, the Wawona

School could well be an example of a functional continuance. Today, Wawona's new school sits on the same site.

Those stalwart early teachers had as much record-keeping to do as they did teaching. And they kept meticulous records, carefully annotating tardy times as well as absences. They listed not only the average daily attendance, but the percentage of attendance. In the 16' x 20' x 12' school, Annie Coughran began her classes with Albert, Jeanie, Hattie and Jay Bruce, with Henry, Frank, May and Lucinda Leonard also in attendance. Clarence Washburn and Joe Amos completed roll call in May 1895.

The father of the four Leonard children was Archie Leonard, who later became one of Yosemite's first rangers. Joe Amos came from the Indian camp at the base of Chowchilla Mountain and Clarence Washburn was the son of John and Estella of the Hotel.

Two years later in May 1897, Katie Leidig, daughter of early area pioneers, attended.

The following year heard Eddie Bruce answering roll call.

Classes were divided into four categories, listed as A, B. C and D. The prescribed work had to be intense, with reading, spelling, writing, arithmetic and geography part of the curriculum. Drawing and composition work was added on some afternoons. Sentences were analyzed and parts of speech defined. Muscular movement with writing was noted.

In 1898, eleven-year-old Thornton Kinney was in school. His parent was listed as Mr. Kinney from Los Angeles, which seemed to bear out the fact that tourist children attended school there in those summer months. Whether this was willing or unwilling attendance was the only thing omitted from the records.

Long lists of visitors were carefully maintained. They came from as close as Wawona and as far away as Honolulu. Sarah L. Washburn visited from Putney, Vermont and Mrs. Bright Gillispie from Wawona. Daisy Degnan from Yosemite Valley visited on May 16, 1898, returning for another look the next day. Lottie Bruce of San Francisco visited the following month and Miss Anna Hill of Wawona dropped by. And so it was verified that the Wawona School offered prime interest in the neighborhood.

Charlie Murphy homesteaded on Chowchilla Mountain, building Deer Glen, his home, and a store. His stepsons, Thomas and John Quillinan, entered first and second grades on May 16, 1910. By this time, Robert Bruce, Azelia's youngest, was in seventh grade.

In 1920, James and Elsie Fulmer spent their first Wawona winter in The White House. The family ranch in Lompoc had been sold and James moved his family in a horse-drawn covered wagon to the mountains. By the following summer, they had moved to Camp Chilnualna where James worked at the Bruce Brothers Sawmill with his team of horses. He later bought packs from Thornton Jackson and began his own brand of tourism by taking tourists into the High Sierra.

Soon after James Fulmer entered Wawona's life stream, he started his own pack station to take tourists on fishing expeditions into the back country. *(Malcolm Fulmer Collection.)*

By 1924, they had purchased one and a quarter acres of land from Albert Spelt and built a home there. In the summers, the pack station was operational and in the winters trapping bear, coyotes, foxes, bobcats and skunks brought them the bounty offered.

Son Malcolm entered school with Albert Gordon, his new and lasting friend. The two soon discovered that they had been born on the same day. Malcom resides today on his ranch near Raymond.

A few years later a little problem nagged at Hattie Spelt's younger daughter, Roberta, when the family moved to San Francisco for the winter. Having finished her semester at Wawona, she was terrified the Truant Officer would come knocking at the door!

In 1937, a new school was dedicated. Lawrence C. Merriam, Acting Superintendent of Yosemite National Park sent his regrets in writing that he could not attend, but sent John B. Wosky, his assistant. Mrs. William Bruce called the Dedication to order, and this was a fitting honor. In time over forty Bruce children would attend school in Wawona with several Bruce parents taking the position of Trustee.

Building the Indian Bridge, about 1920. Once located in the Albert and Azelia Bruce homestead area, but no longer spanning the South Fork. The massive granite in the background has a smooth cavity that attests to years of acorn-pounding by the resident Indians. Second from the left, Albert Spelt. Straddling the log is Jim Fulmer; sitting on the log are Bert Hoyle and Clarence Washburn. Bert Bruce is second from the right. Ed Davey stands at the lower right. Ernest Hoyle stands at the lower left. *(Roberta Bruce Phillips Collection.)*

11 Sons of Chilnualna

February 25, 1895

One last child came along to Azelia and Albert. He was Robert Ingersoll. Albert was then fifty-eight, Azelia forty-five.

Even at two, Robert Bruce seemed to have a musical interest. Above him hangs Azelia's picture of the Three Brothers, and to the left stands a portrait of his father, Albert Olcott. *(Bruce Family Collection.)*

In that same year, John Conway, a master road builder in the area, completed the trail to the upper Chilnualna Falls. The trail to the lower fall had been built earlier by Albert, Ed Washburn and a group of Chinese laborers.

Diligence and everlasting fortitude had given Azelia and Albert a secure homestead and a good life at Wawona. Their family was now complete. Bert, their oldest, was already sixteen. The brood was growing up.

Being established with both homestead and em-ployment could not completely erase Albert's interest in mining and his keen desire to find the mother lode and own a 5-stamp mill. Perhaps he always remembered that rich vein he'd been done out of when little Charlie died, and felt another might be within his reach.

Talk of gold mines and the rich hopes they carried ran through so many veins in Wawona that stage driver, Tom Gordon, was once compelled to comment on the probability: "There isn't five dollars worth a week around." Although nearby Mt. Raymond was pocked with several claims, no one was getting rich.

With the true characteristics of the Forty-niner, Albert refused to abandon hope and remained certain that his fortune was sure to come. He had the faith, and on September 4, 1895, he held in hand a valuable receipt:

Know all persons by these presents that I, R. S. Wellman, have this day of above date sold and conveyed to A. O. Bruce for the sum of five hundred dollars U. S. Gold Coin in hand paid one third interest in a certain Gold and Silver bearing quartz vein situated at the headwaters of the South Fork of the Merced River known as the Condor Mine. The receipt of which is hereby acknowledged.

Robt. S. Wellman
Witness By: John Van Campen
John E. ——(illegible)

Fourth of July Celebration, 1894

This day's gala was an opportunity or tragedy, depending on who was doing the estimation. To thirteen-year-old Jay Cook Bruce, it came as a golden opportunity of which he may have been dreaming. He was making a firecracker when it exploded, leaving his hands and fingers tender and stiff. He somehow persuaded his mother that holding a pencil and books would be impossible for him, and therefore, schooling from that point on would be difficult.

When he was nine, his father had decided he was old enough to learn about guns. He built him a .32 caliber cap and ball revolver, taught him how to make the bullets and showed him how to shoot. Now, Jay's hands seemed to be made for the fishing pole and the gun, if not for pencil and books. He became an outstanding fisherman, and when the family's appetite for fish had run its course, the tourists supplied him with a steady market.

Landscape artist Thomas Hill, who maintained his studio a few feet below the Hotel, decided he would like to dine on quail a couple of times each week, and Jay obliged his palate. For this purpose, Hill loaned the boy his .22 caliber rifle, and was supplied for the season with this culinary delight. When the artist left for San Diego in the fall, he made a gift of the rifle to Jay.

William (Bill), Jeanette, Robert, Edward, and Harriet Bruce of Chilnualna Park in Wawona, about 1898. *(Bruce Family Collection.)*

The presence of the Cavalry in the midst of Wawona's life stream was destined to invoke both sorrow and gladness. In 1896, tragedy, begotten by the homesickness of a young horse soldier, struck a blow. A White Ribboner (non-drinker), Private Chattem Rochette, originally from Wisconsin, allowed several of his buddies to persuade him to take a few drinks at the Hotel store/bar. He was leading the Captain's one-eyed horse back to headquarters when, just after crossing the covered bridge, the one-eyed horse stumbled and fell on Rochette. The trooper's chest was crushed, leaving him with a night of dreadful agony. He died the following day. The military held a funeral with honors. His horse was draped in black, his boots placed backwards in the stirrups and the local children gathered flowers to cover his grave in the cemetery.

Albert felt the death as keenly as though the young man were his own son, prompting him to stoutly declare: "I will never sell another drop of liquor." With that firm pronouncement, he left the

bar business and went back to work at the blacksmith shop welding tires for the stage. His age was no barrier. About thirty years later, Rochette's body was sent back to Wisconsin.

On the happier side, a bevy of the troops often met at the Bruce home and were always welcome. This was practically all the social life enjoyed by these men so far away from home. Musicals were a favorite, with many of the young men gifted with fine voices, and one in particular, Amos Kinzer, talented on the piano.

Once a season the troops were given a special treat. The Bruce girls baked a bunch of cakes, and with freezers of ice cream in tow, Azelia, Jeanie and Harriet would go to the encampment and, serve each man ice cream and cake on Azelia's special glass ice cream dishes that Albert had brought her at the same time as the grand piano from the Judge Grant Hotel.

The troops were extended other courtesies. They were allowed garden plots on the Bruce land

and some even raised hogs on an allotted parcel of land. Small wonder Azelia and Albert were quickly embraced with the loving sobriquet of "Mother and Father of the Army" by the grateful troops.

Just as Azelia was recognized as a woman of many accomplishments, Albert, too, wore many hats. He had learned about machinery, becoming a master at engineering. He had endured the most harsh of conditions in countless mines in the county and as far away as Nevada. Settled at his homestead, he worked diligently at the Washburn blacksmith shop and sawmill.

When the Cavalry marched in, he was soon to walk an additional path. The Army doctors were allowed to treat only their own men, but one of them, Dr. Hall, showed faith in Albert by giving him splints and a medical kit to treat the injured. Some were sheepherders, who fell victim to new policies and new ways imposed by the troops determined to honor their assignment.

Albert had rendered assistance to a Hotel guest suffering from "black fever" and was rewarded by the unfortunate man's mother.

TO ALBERT BRUCE
In grateful remembrance of the sympathy shown and
Kindly assistance rendered to
GEORGE DALZIEL DALZIEL OCTOBER 1884
The gift of his mother.

Presented to him was a handsome clock, about half the size of a shoe box entirely of glass, with its inner workings showcased on four sides, and with the preceding inscription engraved upon it.

Poet, gifted with words he was unafraid to use, inventor, respected father, Albert broadened his field of expertise even more. He once aided in perpetuating the Leidig family dynasty with his help in the elopement of Jack Leidig's mother. He held the ladder while George Leidig sat in the buggy, ready at the reins to make a fast getaway with his intended bride.

Though Azelia taught all her children music, it was the boys who best absorbed the sounds. Eddie enjoyed a gloriously full and golden voice, which could be heard all over Wawona.

Bert grew up with the local Indian boys as his playmates. Fishing and hunting were second na-

Albert Henry (Bert) Bruce could play his fiddle as well as pose with it. *(Skookie Gartin Collection.)*

ture to him, as were both the dangers and beauties of the Sierra.

He inherited the Bruce expertise for the mechanical and scientific and developed an interest in photography which comprised a large portion of his life's work, as well as adding enjoyment for the tourists.

Before radio was available to the public in general, he was involved with that instrument and presented nephew, William Wallace II, with a crystal set of his own invention, which was, in actuality, a radio. A little cat whisker was required to move around on the crystal and the radio was listened to with a pair of headphones. He then developed a peanut tube radio, endowed with a bit more power but still requiring the headphones for sound. Next he developed a battery pack radio for the whole family to enjoy. The old super hetrodyne, his nephew called it, with three dials in the front, which howled at you when trying to tune in.

Bert had antennas in all those tall pine trees

around the house and received from all over the country, his two favorites being KSL in Salt Lake City and a station in Rio Rita Beach in Mexico. A true pioneer in radio, he made all his own parts, with the exception of the tubes.

Until a school was built when he was thirteen, he was home-schooled by his mother. Music, books and arguing were integral parts of growing up in that household.

Interest and abilities ran a happy and parallel course in his life. As a youngster he worked at the Hotel, as did his siblings, and later, though under-age, served as bartender in the Army cantina, which had been erected to keep the troops away from hard liquor.

Photography, though, became his greatest passion, and he became a professional at fourteen. By the age of eighteen, he was surveying for the Cavalry as that body set out to establish boundaries of the National Park. He photographed all the lakes in the high country, as well as the Minarets.

It was the Wawona Tunnel Tree, which became his chief source of income for years, as he captured with his camera scores of happy tourists as they either entered or exited the huge tree which had a passageway sculpted through its great girth. He looked like Wild Bill Hickok. For a memorable photo, he once posed C Troop of the Fourth Cav-

Though flood-damaged, the Wawona covered bridge was renovated to allow passage from today into yesterday. *(Roberta Bruce Phillips Collection.)*

alry on the Fallen Monarch. Even fallen, the giant tree dwarfed the men. He also snapped the six-horse stage with Henry Washburn, Thomas Hill and Ed Baxter (grandson of John J. Cook), at one time a Guardian of the Grove, atop the fallen sequoia to again immortalize men and tree with a photograph. The pictures became events, prized through the succeeding years.

From Bert's photographic work came a business in postcards, as he and Charlie Stephan developed a line of them for the tourist trade.

It could have been all those books in the family library, filled with so many facts, that inspired the children in their differing opinions. They argued, and often the arguments led to spirited fights. But Bert seldom had a word to say against anyone. He was like stage driver, Eddie Gordon, in that respect. Rather than engage in spirited conflict, his attitude was *"Oh, the hell."* In this family of vigorous arguers, Bert was the most easy-going.

On February 7, 1904, he married Martha Marian Laird and they moved to Mt. Bullion where he worked at the Mount Gaines Mine. There he kept his camera handy to record the workers, their functions and the territory.

Albert Henry Bruce, at right, with a tourist in the era when Bert looked like Wild Bill Hickok—at least to some of his family. *(Morrie Bruce Collection.)*

68

The Wawona Civilian Conservation Corps camp from 1933 to 1942. The CCC boys showed expertise and hard work in cleaning up after the loggers and in building bridges and other structures. *(Skookie Gartin Collection.)*

On Christmas Day 1905, he wrote from Mt. Bullion that his job of firing at the mine was tough since all the wood was green. By the following year, he had become a father, naming his son Albert, after his pa. Pride besotted him when he wrote his mother that the baby was "as bright as a new silver dollar and gains a pound a week."

William Wallace, most often known as Bill, and as Willie by his mother, inherited the building ability of both his father and mother's family. They were all builders and wheelwrights engaged in the construction processes, and Bill followed the family tradition with his work in Yosemite Valley. There he helped rebuild the ranger station and bridges, and at Wawona worked with the Civilian Conservation Corps, teaching the young men all he knew about building.

At Wawona's Seventh Day Adventist Camp, he worked on various construction projects with Albert Gordon, who said

If the hint of a smile on Jay Cook Bruce's face spells satisfaction, his bag for the day gives credence to it. *(Bruce Family Collection.)*

of him, "He was the most honest man I ever worked with."

Though Bill had dark eyes and his father blue eyes, a visiting Scotsman once made the terse remark that he was the ridiculous image of his father.

Jay Cook Bruce was a mountain man. It was propitious that his father had taught him the intricacies of guns and hunting, and through his friendship with an Indian boy named Joe Amos, learned to use bow and arrows and the art of tracking. The main body of his life was shaped.

By the time he was an old man, Jay could look back with the utmost satisfaction and think, yes, I have done it all. He had been successful in his career as the official State Cougar Hunter, had made movies, put on shows with his cougar cubs, written a 172-page book, testimony in itself that the Bruce way with words had been passed down, and he had married a woman he loved. Hardly could his esteemed father have said more of himself.

Jay heeded an old advice for business success, which proclaimed: "Find a need and fill it." It could be said his business career began on that fateful Fourth of July when the firecracker injured his hand and he prevailed upon his mother to allow him to drop out of school.

In subscribing to his own business philosophy, in a two-year period, he caught 32,000 trout and sold them to the Washburns for the dining pleasure of the Hotel guests. But that lucrative enterprise ended when the State Legislature, with the governor's signature, passed a law banning the sale of trout.

When the Washburns were asked by the Congressman of the Wawona District to recommend someone for either West Point or Annapolis, the brothers selected Jay, even offering to pay his expenses while attending. Jay turned down the offer.

Forest Townsley, of the National Park Service in Yosemite Valley, obtained for him a forestry lease on Camp A. E. Wood for one hundred dollars per year. Instead of exercising that option, he borrowed money to acquire horses and became a hunting and fishing guide, a job entirely to his liking, though seasonal and benefiting him with only a small earning. To supplement this, he played the mandolin at the Music Hall, located near the Hotel. The chords invariably attracted a score of dancers.

Having managed to save some money by 1906, he enrolled in the Heald School of Mines and Engineering. Unfortunately, this phase of Jay's life and ambition was abruptly brought to a halt by the great San Francisco earthquake and fire which destroyed the school.

Back to the mountains. From the Mt. Gaines Mine in Mt. Bullion, where he found work, he wrote that he was studying books on surveying that had been sent him and planned on returning to San Francisco to continue his studies in assaying and surveying. It was June 1906, and the earthquake had only delayed, not defeated him.

Bert's marriage was in trouble.

On May 2, 1910, Azelia wrote about the trouble to Hattie. She had just returned from Mariposa in a surrey with a team of horses supplied by Ed Washburn. "We went in style as surrey had just been painted and varnished," she proudly stated. There was no one to meet her since both Jay and Willie were in Mt. Bullion at an Odd Fellows celebration. They both had taken three degrees.

Albert Olcott Bruce, grandson of Azelia and Albert, with his mother, Martha Marian. After a bitter court battle, his care was turned over to Azelia.
(Morrie Bruce Collection.)

She had gone to Mariposa to support Bert in his divorce and custody battle with his wife, Marian. "Trabucco will take a month to decide as he wants to look up some points in the case," she informed her daughter, going on to say that the lady in contestation was represented by two lawyers, Adair and Beardsley, who started off with a big hurrah, but soon found out they were on the wrong side of the case!

Lawyers and Azelia alike stopped at Schlageter's Hotel while in Mariposa.

Little Albert, four years old, was with his father. His mother's lawyer told the court that he would give Bert his bond for the return of the child and also pay any young lady the court might designate to stay with him. But Bert insisted that his son stay with Azelia through the night, being returned in the morning. Judge Trabucco ordered a schedule for the boy, which stated that he should be in his grandmother's custody for part of the day. Clearly, it was a tug of war which Marian's lawyer hoped to bring to a sensational conclusion. But the boy fooled them. He yelled his head off. "I want my Grandma, I want my Papa!" And he kept this up until his mother was happy to fetch him back. Everybody in town heard about it and half the townsfolk heard the yelling.

Excited groups of Mariposa's population stood at every gate Azelia afterwards passed, and they were all desirous to know what became of the boy.

Marian had not mustered a good defense. Her own mother did not show up, and her only witness, Logan Duncan, soon deserted her by saying, "I do not know how any man could take her back after what she did."

The real tearjerker was a letter Bert had written his wife after the divorce case, and which Marian had, for some unknown reason, brought along to court. It was a beautiful letter, and when read in court, didn't leave a dry eye. It even left Jay and Eddie crying.

Having custody of young Albert was a major triumph for Azelia, as well as for Bert. Her years were advancing, and she often felt "bum" and wished for two better legs upon which to stand, but she welcomed her grandson.

Wawona May 10, 1910

Albert had been ill for over a year and Azelia's own health was worsening. Only a few days after the fateful trial in Mariposa, she wrote Hattie that she was literally on her last legs. The sciatica rheumatism, as she labeled her condition, left her unable to move a muscle without screaming. But there was a lot left to do and a tremendous amount of enthusiasm to take her there.

Jay was getting married. He had, in fact, left the previous day for Fresno to meet his bride, Katherine Fournier of Mariposa, whom he would wed in two days. Willie had just arrived to stay with his mother for a short time and gave his appraisal of Jay's intended. Katherine was a sweet girl, he attested. Azelia had a somewhat acerbic comment to make about the girl's relationship. It was laced with a little leftover triumph from the courtroom saga. Jay's bride was motherless, a condition Azelia favored with words to Hattie: "So thank God there will be no mother-in-law to interfere." A more attributable aspect of the relationship was her worship of Jay. About his intended, Jay insisted that "She was the only girl that never tried to deceive him about anything."

With the impending marriage, Azelia had to forget the misery in her bones and, in her words, "rake up some presents."

First, she sent for a Battinburg scarf. In her stores, she had a lovely lace bed set, a bride's set, which she lined with bird's egg blue. She made a beautiful black pin cushion which she covered with point desprite lace and edged with ruffles. It was an elegant pincushion with rows of blue ribbons and studded with faux diamonds that Hattie had given her.

Azelia did not stop there. Her happiness in Jay's marriage showed itself in her further collection of wedding gifts. She gave them curtains, a pair of blue and gold vases, two cushion tops of Jay's selection, six silver knives, six forks, six tablespoons, 12 teaspoons and a butter knife. She gave them a silver cake tray and cream ladle and three table-cloths, all hand-hemmed. And she had done all this sewing and readying for his great day since her return of only a few days earlier from Mariposa.

She went on to write Hattie: "I also tucked by hand the whole front of one of those beautiful hand-embroidered waists for her."

Jay was, she declared, the backbone of the family and she felt far happier about his marriage than that of Bert. Her words were scornful of Bert's wife, whose own lawyer had told her to get out of Mariposa as fast as God would let her. The Bruce's lawyer, John Wall, "roasted La Fleur on the stand, leaving her white as a sheet and shaking like a leaf. Her determination to make Bert wish he had never been born went seriously awry and Bert came out like pure gold from the furnace of fire," Azelia wrote.

Of Jay, Hattie once wrote; "Jay resembled Mother's side of the family and therefore he was her favorite."

There was no doubt that Azelia was Bert's mother, as well as Jay's.

Times were lean, with winter leaner than summer. Eddie had made $120 for the whole of the previous year.

It was perhaps, inevitable that Azelia's life should be somewhat patterned after an opera. In tragic operas recounting great epics, there is often a crescendo of lilting, joyous music immediately preceding the weepy end.

Though she was far from feeling the sprightly young self she had so long enjoyed, her darling Jay's marriage filled her with delight. She had Eddie at home, as well as teenager Bob and Willie dropped in from time to time. She had been entrusted with the raising of young Albert. Her life was full and exceptionally busy.

And then the shutters were drawn. An era closed down.

In his long life, Albert had worked diligently. He had filed a dozen mining claims, worked with acknowledged efficiency on the machinery of countless mines, patented his own inventions, worked in a sawmill, a bar and a store. He raised wheat and hay and seven children, and in those seven children, forged a future where he would not be forgotten. He loved one woman with a passion and, with the soul of a poet, he embraced her with faithful letters and undying devotion.

Though it might have been the time of his choosing, it was also a time when too many miseries were suffered rather than cured. Penicillin and streptomycin were wonders not yet known. He had been ill for two years when, on February 21, 1911, he left his beloved homestead forever, victim of paralysis. John Davis was visiting Archie Leonard when the two were called to the Bruce homestead by Albert's son, Edward. Albert had died at four that afternoon. John Davis, with Bright Gillespie, prepared the remains for transport to Mariposa. Albert was then placed in a box and taken by sled to Mariposa, where he was buried in the Mariposa I. O. O. F. Cemetery two days later.

Years before, on the 22nd day of July 1885, the Declaration of Homestead had been filed in the office of the County Recorder of Mariposa County. Now, Azelia petitioned to have the real property vested in her name. It was done by Judge J. J. Trabucco on September 29, 1913.

Other changes were imminent. In the summer of 1912, Jay and Bert built a sawmill, the object being to cut lumber to build rental cabins on the homestead property and sell the surplus to interested buyers. Upon Jay's insistence, they started with a Franklin Flyer,[1] which in time failed to meet the sawmill's needs. This method of operation was soon replaced, as was the argumentative Jay. It was decided to use a Pelton Wheel, which was water powered. A flume was then constructed, running from Chilnualna Creek to a point above the mill. A tank was installed to collect the water and a pipe

The Pelton Wheel was operated by water pressure. To power the water wheel, a flume was constructed from Chilnualna Creek to 200 feet above the Bruce sawmill. The Pelton Water Wheel also generated electricity. Today it is on display at the Wawona History Center. *(Photo by Thomas Bruce Phillips.)*

brought the water to the Pelton Wheel to power the saw.

Jay later built another sawmill and produced lumber that went into the construction of additional buildings for the Hotel. Fire destroyed this mill in 1915.

Bert, Bill and Bob later ran the family sawmill, with the bulk of the lumber sold to the Currys in Yosemite Valley. The brothers pioneered the use of knotty pine which was used to build Camp Curry and used some of the lumber to build various cabins for summer rental on their own property.

Foresight kept astride of their innovations. They were the first to practice selective harvesting of the trees. They cut only the mature or bug-infested trees, falling the timber into openings in a careful effort to spare the younger growth. The fallen timber was then hauled to the mill with horses and mule teams on wooden wheeled carts. By 1925, 2,000,000 feet of lumber had gone through their mill.

Hauling the timber on wooden-wheeled wagons, 1920. *(W. Bruce Collection.)*

1. A gasoline powered automobile engine.

The gateway to the Mariposa Grove of Big Trees could well be called the gateway to splendor. Beyond it rose sequoias whose mammoth proportions invoked awe from all who beheld them. The man in the foreground possibly is Ed Baxter, grandson of John J. Cook. *(Catherine Jeanette Stephan/Hartske Collection.)*

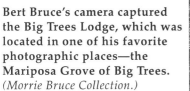

Bert Bruce's camera captured the Big Trees Lodge, which was located in one of his favorite photographic places—the Mariposa Grove of Big Trees. *(Morrie Bruce Collection.)*

Bill and Robert Bruce with their hands full of lumber at the Bruce sawmill. *(W. Bruce Collection.)*

12 Daughters of Chilnualna

Jeanie and Hattie spent their childhood in Wawona, growing up beautiful young ladies. Jeanie, who began calling herself Jeanette, possessed a gift uniquely her own in the uncanny perception she developed. Hattie was to later find her own niche in another mode of communication.

Jeanette Frances Bruce, about 1903, by the garden fence of the homestead house. *(Maddalena Gartin Collection.)*

Hattie Bruce wore a serious expression as she clutched her Aunt Fannie's book of poetry, about 1894. It could be called a prelude to Hattie's long life, with reading an important tool for information. *(Roberta Bruce Phillips Collection.)*

These were the days when the Cavalry was around. Romance began to bloom. The romance involved Trooper Allen Kilgour, and it was not sharply defined in the beginning. Jeanette fancied him, but so did the irrepressible Hattie. One of the girls was bound to lose.

One day Hattie became determined to ride down to camp to see Allen. She jumped on a horse and was ready to sprint when Jeanette whistled. Since it was Jeanette's horse the spirited Hattie was attempting to ride, the horse threw her upon hearing her mistress whistle, and Hattie took a frightful spill. The fall severely damaged her face, requiring Azelia to take her daughter to San Francisco for corrective surgery.

By the time she was eighteen, Jeanette was the one who had won Allen. Both her parents signed their acceptance of her underage marriage, and on February 16, 1903, she and twenty-three-year-old

Jeanette Bruce and Allen Kilgour on their wedding day. She looks pensive but content, while Allen is focused on the photographer.
(Maddalena Gartin Collection.)

position there. However, she heeded her mother's advice and remained in San Francisco where she went to work for Western Union. Years later, she penned a note to Yosemite Park Naturalist, Douglass H. Hubbard, in which she lamented her voluntary sojourn in the city. "I felt like an exile in a strange land and I longed for the day when I would return to my hills."

She may have longed for her beloved Wawona, but Hattie built a reputation with Western Union, which would outlast her days. For many years, in the time of the old hand key, she was one of the fastest telegraphers in the San Francisco office. And when she was twenty-two, she put her wide mountain experience to good use. It was April 18, 1906, and the city had just been devastated by an earthquake and fire. Hattie climbed a telephone pole, tied her key across the wires and sent out the first message about the disaster to the other part of the world.

Claimed also in that terrible calamity was the Taber Studio. This photographic studio, which had pioneered the 3-D photo enhancement, and in which John Jay Cook was part owner, was wiped out in the fire.

Hattie did have her observations, and they could include her kin as well as outsiders. She said once of her aunt, Catherine Leitch: "Dear old Aunt

Allen were married at St. John's Rectory in San Francisco by Louis Childe Sanford, the Rector.

Edward Washburn saw in Hattie a great potential and encouraged her to attend Heald Business School in San Francisco to study telegraphy. Upon her return to the mountains, he advised her, she could become stenographer, bookkeeper and telegrapher at the Hotel. Hattie did heed his advice, but upon her return in 1903, that position was already filled by Daisy Degnan.

John J. Cook's son, Hattie's cousin, Jay B. Cook, was then manager of the Sentinel Hotel in Yosemite Valley. He was also the postmaster. The Wells Fargo telegraph office was located in the Sentinel, and Hattie was offered a

The Palace Hotel in its death throes dealt by the San Francisco earthquake and fire of 1906. From a 1906 postcard.
(Roberta Bruce Phillips Collection.)

Catherine Bruce Leitch's portrait was taken sometime before the 1906 earthquake and fire destroyed the Taber Studio. The studio was partly owned by her brother-in-law, John Jay Cook. His investment was completely lost. *(Bruce Family Collection.)*

Bruce Mitchel Leitch, son of Catherine and Bruce Leitch. He wrote *Big Trees of California,* published in 1910, a booklet embellished with splendid pictures of the Mariposa Grove. Captain Benson of the Cavalry spoke highly of his stewardship of the Grove. I. W. Taber photo. *(Roberta Bruce Phillips Collection.)*

Kate. If she did nothing else, she taught me the proper way to drag a half train across our mud and snow splattered floor."

Acting Superintendent Harry Benson held a more generous opinion of Catherine's son, Bruce Mitchel Leitch Jr. At one time the younger Bruce operated a curio shop in the Mariposa Grove and served at one time as a Grove Guardian. In 1906, Benson described him as "the only person in the Mariposa Grove whose presence helps secure the place and who was able to answer tourist questions and add greatly to the visitors' pleasure."

He also served as the mail carrier between Mariposa and Big Tree Station. The times seemed to demand versatility in a man.

Hattie was hearing wedding bells. She had met James Spelt in the city, and he was The One.

Azelia had a few words on the subject of Hattie's plans to wed. "You certainly have courage," her mother wrote, "with Jen's example before you." (Jeanette's marriage to Allen Kilgour was dissolving.) "But suppose you will never be satisfied until, like Eve, you taste the apple. Well, you must give me more time than Jay did. I think October a lovely month to be married. Only wish you could come home for two weeks, if no more."

Hattie chose not to wait until fall. On July 10, 1910, she married James Albert Spelt.

Exactly when Jeanette fully realized what lay within her in a spiritual or psychic sense can't be tracked. Doubtlessly, some power lurked there, latent, but ready to be tapped. She would become a spiritualist minister, often telling fortunes, investing into this extra sense in a more powerful and meaningful way than had her uncle, Robert Kale, been able to manage.

Living in San Francisco after her marriage, she advertised as a psychic, and the people came.

In the early 1930s, on the occasion of a return to Wawona, she was readying for a spiritual meeting when thirteen-year-old Albert Gordon lingered by the open doorway. "Come on in, boy," she invited. Terrified by what he could not understand, Albert fled to the relative safety of hotel owner, Clarence Washburn's nearby office.

This 1904 photo of Harriet Bruce shows none of the fire in her spirit that would later ignite when she set the record straight.
(Roberta Bruce Phillips Collection.)

13 Winding Down

From Scartho House in Grimsby, England, came this letter of recommendation on October 6, 1913:

> I have known Miss Hall for several years and can vouch for the integrity of her character. She is conscientious and thoroughly trustworthy. She is capable of filling a position of trust, and would be thoroughly honorable in all her dealings.
>
> E. P. Eason.

Miss Ada Hall went to Wawona to become nanny to Jeanette's children. They are Donald, Muriel, Hester, and Alberta Kilgour. *(Skookie Gartin Collection.)*

Miss Hall was Miss Ada Hall, more lately of Victoria, Canada, and her destiny was in the works when Azelia, desperately needing help, hired her as a nanny.

Azelia was in a turmoil of worries. Her will was stronger than her heartbeat, and she feared she was suffering heart failure as well as the crippling rheumatism.

Allen Kilgour had left Jeanette with their four children to raise, and those children were now in Azelia's care. Three of the children came down with the measles, Willie sitting up with them for several nights to relieve Miss Hall. Donald was full of the Old Nick and impossible to keep in the house. And he needed new shoes.

Azelia suffered other worries. Bert was injured, and although both Willie and Bob were with him at the Mountain King Mine, she fretted that she was unable to go to him, and that he might be neglected.

Ada Hall Bruce and William W. Bruce. Ada went from being a nanny to become a true daughter of Chilnualna when she married Willie Bruce. *(Bruce Family Collection.)*

On the bright side, an eight-passenger Thomas was purchased, and just in time for the big event. On November 17, in the year 1914, Willie and Ada Hall were married in the Mariposa Hotel, by Justice of the Peace W. A. Scott. The Mariposa Hotel was formerly known as the Schalgeter Hotel, where his mother and father were married many years before. Azelia wrote: "We went to Mariposa in auto, got license, got married, took our dinner and came back in time for supper." It was a busy day.

Ada Hall's sister, May, captured the heart of Eddie Bruce, but the romance was not to be.
(Bruce Family Collection.)

Another telling tale was set down. Ada had a sister. In May, May Hall was coming from England, and Ada and Willie went to San Francisco to meet her. The date of Eddie's destiny lay not too far in the future. He fell in love with May.

For money, Eddie trapped. On December 13, 1915, he wrote his mother, who was in San Francisco with Hattie, that he had trapped two wild cats and a skunk. After the first of the year, the wild cat bounty would be raised to $50, a tempting price for

any trapper. The lions were prevalent in those years. At the nearby Sugar Pine Mill, nine of them were trapped in the year past.

It was fortuitous that Azelia, in her older years, could winter in a more temperate place than Wawona and that Hattie welcomed both her and Azelia's youngest, Bob.

Bob got a job with the Bulletin, soliciting advertisements. For each dollar value, he made 25¢. At the same time, Jeanette worked at the Emporium for $40 per month, and Hattie still worked for Western Union.

These men cutting ice on Stella Lake earned $2.50 per day and two pairs of woolen gloves. Pictured are Art Gallison, Charles Fobes, Lynn Butler with his dog, Bouie Ashworth, Eddie Gordon with a proud dog, Jack Davis, and two unknowns.
(Bruce Family Collection.)

Winter wore on with Eddie alone on the homestead. He worked cutting ice on Stella Lake, a Washburn enterprise that kept the Hotel in ice for the coming summer. During this time he bunked in the powerhouse with Arthur Gallison, a young man who also worked at Wawona, cutting ice in winter and at the Hotel in summer. Art would become one of Yosemite's first rangers the next year, serving at the Alder Creek entrance station.

As winter dragged on, Eddie measured the two more months he had to stick around as years. He was twenty-four years old and ready for some of life's little perks.

Willie and Ada were at Melones, his mother and younger brother in San Francisco, as were his two sisters. May was working in a private sanitarium, and although he heard from her, he was plagued with loneliness.

The weather was at its meanest, the worst winter Eddie had endured. Three feet and four inches of snow piled up and then the temperature plummeted to ten below. When the clouds rolled in, it rained six inches within 12 hours. He lamented, in a letter, that he had made only $7 on the ice-cutting job and could not even check his traps because of the storms.

He wrote frequently to his sister-in-law, Ada, of whom he was very fond. It also gave him ways to hear of his beloved May. He was extremely anxious to get to the city to see her, but doubted if he could before fall. And this was early March. He was also anxious to find work, possibly at Melones where Brother Willie worked. His goal was to put aside $200 by fall, a desire aligned with his hope for May's hand.

Azelia put her homestead on the

Azelia Van Campen Bruce sat behind her homestead house. She would have to feel content with her life's achievements. *(Morrie Bruce Collection.)*

market. If it sold, she reasoned, there was the possibility that the new owner would build rental cottages on the land, with this venture offering employment to a considerable force of men. Eddie was hopeful.

But the place did not sell and Azelia would soon be in residence once more and needing help to fix it up. Eddie knew he was the elected one and felt resentful that it should be he, rather than Bob, to have to stay on when he had just endured a nasty winter there. After all, he wrote Ada, Bert and Bob had declared they wouldn't stay there for a thousand dollars!

And then a touchy thing happened. Eddie expected his mother to sell the place for $35,000 and share with him a part of the proceeds he felt were his due. After all, he had wintered there alone, caring for the premises. He advised Willie to seek the same, going on to say:

> I suppose you know what Ma has done to me, after I being so good as to stay in here for her. So I feel she owes me something tho she can never pay me for the misery she has caused me. If we get our share we can put in together and get a home so we can have that much even tho I can never be happy again.

What had happened? What could his mother have done to so embitter Eddie? Those closest to the scene were certain that Azelia had squashed Eddie's romance with May. And he was hard pushed to forgive her this transgression.

Those sentiments were set down on March 31, 1916, when Eddie went on to inform his brother that he had been busy cleaning up the place and had it looking in tip-top shape.

But when Azelia arrived home three weeks later she viewed the place through different eyes. She was, at this time, hovering around sixty-six years of age. Her health was deteriorating, and as she looked around her house, barely able to breathe, she knew she would never be able to live there again. She saw the oilcloth on the table as black as the stove. The floor was dirty. She saw neglect that she termed squalor. She worried that she would never be able to haul over the groceries. But worst of all there was no wood cut!

Jay was then working for Ed Baxter at the Big

Trees and had hiked down to build a fire for her, but he arrived 25 minutes too late. The house was icily cold.

Eddie left. He had told Jay that he had to get out or lose his girl. Still determined to keep May, he then found work with the stage company.

Through the years, the friendship of Azelia and Adelia Swaney had endured. Though Adelia's own health was often precarious, she corresponded with her old friend with an optimistic spirit, laced with hopes that Azelia would soon visit her in San Francisco. She added the inducement of Nat Haskell's expected visit at Christmas time. In early October he sailed for China as the engineer aboard the *Great Republic* and was to return on December 20 with hopes of seeing again the now-single Azelia.

Andy Swaney sent his love to Azelia, telling his wife to make "the bushels" of it "in good shape." And so she did, embellishing her letter above her signature with fluffy circles, a trademark of hers.

It was countdown time to a disaster that no one could have suspected. On October 22, 1916, a crestfallen Eddie shot himself. He was only twenty-five. Despite his perseverance and efforts to save money,

he had lost his darling May to another man. Gone now was the golden voice so often heard around Wawona, and gone was Azelia's hope, so often laced with despair, that he would help her ready her place for immediate sale.

Azelia's despair only deepened. Her art gave her a modicum of surcease as she painted a picture of Mt. Raymond, companion piece to her Bald Rock painting. She also had a commission from Patti Uhl for a painting. However much her art gave balm to her misery, she saw her health worsening with terrible pain in her head and throat, incessant since Eddie's death. She would never recover from the dreadful loss.

March of 1917 saw conditions at Wawona and Azelia's home grow even more bleak. Storms beset the area, the Worman boys had not been able to carry the mail for a week and the household was on the "shorts." Azelia was grateful for Willie's money order. Bob swore he would never spend another winter there or he would be taken out in a box. Added to the mother's worries was Jeanette's bout with tonsillitis. Her sorrows never came single file.

Willie was devoted to his mother. He was still working as bookkeeper at Melones in Calaveras

Believed to be in Melones. Both Bert and Willie Bruce worked there. The area is now under water.
(Bruce Family Collection.)

Azelia Villette Van Campen Bruce, a lady who more than matched her name. Both heartache and triumph visited her life, but she always persevered. *(Roberta Bruce Phillips Collection.)*

County, his wife was expecting a baby, but still he managed to send a money order to his mother. But on April 16, 1917, Bob had managed to find work, easing their situation, and she implored Willie to keep his money. Both she and Bob were very saving, he being, in her words, "a fright over it."

The only fresh meat of the entire winter was made available when Bob and Jay killed two big bears. Additionally, Jay killed two lions in the Devil's Gulch country. Azelia tried a little bear meat for breakfast, but was not too keen on it, and though Jay had rendered 20 pounds of lard from the bears, her stomach did protest at the thought of that lard, she confided in one of her letters.

The snow did not know spring from winter. A foot could fall, and did, in a 24-hour period. There was still five feet on the summit, and the severe cold made Azelia utterly miserable. Her desire to sell by summer was intensified, and her thoughts of warmer climates took her to Los Angeles or San Diego.

Of an historical nature, the Mt. Gaines gold mine at Hornitos, idle for seven years, was expected to become productive again after an infusion of big capital. In its early days, steam power was used for the compressors, but now with electricity doing part of the hoisting and drilling, a more economical venture was conceived. With new machinery installed, the 12-man work force would undoubtedly increase, resulting in a ratio of greater employment, always beneficial to the county.

Then there was the war to worry Azelia. Though she could not understand how it would affect mining operations, the mine at Melones was threatening to close down, and thus Willie's job was in jeopardy. Willie was her angel in human form, always sending her $10 each month.

The Washburn enterprises also seemed to be of an uncertain nature. John Washburn, with his son Clarence, was running the Hotel. Henry had died in 1902, and with his death went the vision. Much of their business was slashed when they were no longer allowed to take passengers into the Valley. Azelia wrote: "They will have nothing to do but collect toll and feed people that come in their private machines." Ways and roads were changing course. Machines came from Merced by way of Miami Lodge and a lunch stop, then on to Fish Camp and Big Trees and Wawona, a long day's drive. Although Azelia was in possession of a $150 check from the Washburns, cashing it had to wait until the business picked up, as was bound to happen, she was confident.

Perhaps it was the influx of workers for the Sugar Pine Mill; perhaps it was sorely missing Eddie, her golden-voiced son, and her own avowed loneliness, but Azelia began to feel afraid, an unsettling condition that she had never before experienced. So she did the practical thing—she got a dog.

It was most likely the times rather than the territory that made such a nervous wreck of her. This war was "so different from the Civil War," she once remarked. The idea of Bob being conscripted set her nerves to the exploding point, for he, too, felt he would be called up. She prayed that God would grant both Willie and Jay exemptions.

She kept abreast of the news when Hattie had the *Examiner* sent to her from San Francisco. She deplored the war, the food shortages. "I can not see the use of starving our own people to send to Europe," she wrote Bert when she could buy only an allotted one dozen cans of milk at Black's and she thought President Wilson a dictator same as the Kaiser and Czar, for his part in the war. Clearly, Azelia entertained strong sentiments.

John Washburn became too ill to travel from San Francisco, where he wintered, to Wawona to handle the business, and Azelia feared this was "the end of him."

Selling her homestead was of prime consideration. Bob Sherman, a wealthy man who was head of the Tijon Cattle Company and owned cattle ranches in Idaho and Montana, as well as a huge acreage put to beans, might be her salvation. He had just purchased an additional 28,000 acres and was interested in buying Azelia's property. She fervently hoped he would, but if he did not, her old tenacity was alive and ready to be activated. She would put the land to potatoes, that staple being so high. One thought was invariable: she could never again spend a winter at Wawona.

This slab cabin, graced with the name "Laurel," was one of Albert Spelt's Chilnualna cabins. *(Courtesy of Norman May.)*

14 The Man Who Went To War

Another Fourth of July.

"Lafayette, we are here," spoke Colonel Charles E. Stanton on this day in 1917, as he stood before the tomb of Lafayette.

For the United States, this road to France had begun to be traveled on an unalterable course a few months previous, on April 6, when both the Senate and House, its members called to special session, voted to enter the war. The vote was inevitable. Only three weeks earlier, German U-boats had sunk the American ships *Illinois* and *City of Memphis,* and after this outrage, the president delivered an impassioned speech before Congress and Supreme Court justices, in which he said in part "we will not choose the path of submission."

The nation was poorly prepared. Troops made only $15 per month, hardly an incentive for enlistment. To soften the sound of it, Conscription was renamed Selective Service, even as its intent remained unchanged. U. S. Secretary of War Newton D. Baker drew the first number in the draft lottery, and the country was on its way to mobilization.

Azelia read everything she could lay her hands on concerning conscription. She was against it. She busied herself advising her sons how to best claim a legitimate exemption. Willie's wife was expecting a child, and additionally, he had always opposed killing, two facts Azelia pointed out. As for Bob, he was her handy crutch upon which to lean.

Something of a lighter note helped Azelia survive that summer of '17. Most of the family's Chilnualna Cottages were full, and one particular family was generous in their hospitality, inviting her to tea, lunch and dinner. The Burness family had brought their own cook from Scotland. Interesting to Azelia, the grandmother of this family was a Jean Bruce of Perth, Scotland and "she looked just like Aunt Kate and Aunt Jean. And she acts like them and her children act just like the Bruce children of the old stock," she wrote Ada.

The Burness children had ten years musical training on different instruments behind them, but they could not compare to Bob, Azelia was proud to add.

Summer wasn't over yet. An old beau dropped by. He had been such a bashful young man, but had certainly changed as he told an astonished Azelia that she was the only woman in the world he had ever loved and had never got over her memory. This declaration had to be close to the truth, for he patted her hands, her cheeks and her hair. She very nearly asked him if he was a lunatic, she later confessed in a letter. The gentleman was then seventy-four.

In a letter of May 1885, an exasperated Albert had responded to some of Azelia's fretting over their long separations. He alluded to the disposition of his hard-earned property should he pass on. "Perhaps for some old one-eyed rancher to enjoy the fruits of my labor." He could rest in peace. Azelia maintained a posture of resistance before this old beau.

Her years were adding on, and her health often dragged her to the limits of desolation, but Azelia could always, always write a keen and informative letter.

Azelia had worries enough in her own domain, but her life had been so well integrated with the Washburns' enterprises that she could not help but continue her concern as trouble brewed there. John Washburn had died, and Henry's daughter, Jeanie, became embroiled in a power play for management. She was at this time Chairman of the Board, with 50 per cent of the stock and wanted control. Azelia, who had spent so many long evenings at her treadle sewing machine hemming Hotel linens, viewed the situation with a candid eye, writing that Jeanie's sister-in-law was "a brazen~faced devil and mischief maker" who was trying to kill Jeanie in order for her brother to gain control.

It was eventually John's son, Clarence, who took over the management.

To complicate her stress, a cousin, Frank Mackie, of Avoca, New York, died and she was entitled to a portion of his estate. The widow's lawyer wrote Azelia that her share would be about $3000, the land being worth about $20 or $25 per acre, he claimed. Azelia suspected trickery since her grand-

The Wawona Tunnel Tree, with a passage sculpted through it, offered a special excitement to tourists who visited the Mariposa Grove of Big Trees. Robert Bruce stood in the back of the wagon. *(Roberta Bruce Phillips Collection.)*

father had paid $75 per acre for land only three miles away, and that was in 1835.

Fearful that his mother would lose everything, Bob planned to go east and look into the matter. Hattie was still with Western Union and Azelia prevailed upon her to learn through a company manager just what the value of Steuben County, New York land was worth. She suspected that her share of this estate, which consisted of three farms on 500 acres, three farm houses, barns and $6400 in personal property, could amount to upwards of $20,000.

By the middle of September that year, Bob had decided the trip would pinch them financially. His mother was beginning to worry that there would not be enough money left in the coffer to bury her.

A 40-room cottage with bathrooms was being built at the Hotel complex. It would be called The Annex and charge $7.50 per day. A golf course and swimming pool were also being developed to encourage

guests to stay and enjoy. With all this building, work would be available for Bob, but he had decided by then to work at ship building in Los Angeles for $6.50 per day. He would not claim an exemption.

As it happened, Bob worked fitting inlet and outlet pipes to the new pool, as well as with Mr. Brinkop, Clarence Washburn's father-in-law, who was installing a steam water system. The men working on The Annex declared that Bob could do anything.

The country had not come up with its quota in the last draft call and another was scheduled for the first of the following year. Azelia hoped for peace before anyone else would be drafted. She wrote Willie that the Japs thought the war would continue for another four years, in which case, she asserted, everyone would starve. "Surely the world is upside down and topsy turvey when you see kings coming to us with hats in hand for our aid."

Then, instead of embarking on the eastern trip to check his mother's inheritance, Bob went into the Army and was stationed at Ft. McDowell.

The property had not sold, but Azelia hoped to

Jeanette Frances Bruce and Robert Ingersoll Bruce astride their steeds in the tall trees. Note that Jeanette rode sidesaddle. *(Bruce Family Collection.)*

The smile on Robert Bruce's face could be attributable to his complete satisfaction with army life, as well as the photographer's command to say "cheese." (*Bruce Family Collection.*)

the Army, but his mother was still concerned that Willie might be drafted and begged him to declare her as a dependent on the pertinent questionnaire.

And she felt her time was short.

It can certainly be said of this pioneer that she persevered. She wrote long letters to her children despite her health. Her quick mind fastened on every event around her. She was often cold, but determined to save coal, she delighted in the enthusiastic letters received from Bob, accepted that he would soon leave for France, and all the while

be out of Wawona by the middle of November before another winter's onslaught would assail her. She began packing her possessions with the idea of moving back to Hattie's in San Francisco. She asked Jeanette to send her two strong bolts with screws so that she might tightly secure her house. She had come to mistrust her beloved Jay who had already helped himself to many of her prized keepsakes.

Christmas neared. Azelia was with Hattie and wishing for her old Wawona home. But her despondency lifted when Bob came marching in on Christmas Eve in his soldier's duds, looking to his mother "a beauty." Her youngest son was delighted with his special branch in the service—telephone and telegraph.

It is probable that her bad health helped her with her worrying. Bob was happy in

Azelia's brush and pen were never still. She painted until a short time before her death. Shown here are her renditions of The Three Graces (top) and The Three Brothers.

she wrote and wrote, apprising her children of just about everything that was going on.

Early in January of the New Year 1918, Bob wrote his mother from Monterey that the military insisted on absolute secrecy as to troop movement, and therefore he could not tell her when or where he would go. He had taken care to provide for her with an insurance policy in case of his death and a monthly assignment of $15 per month, with the government adding $10 for her support. He expected her to receive her first allotment by the middle of February. Sadly, she would never collect it.

Azelia was sure that Bob was all that was needed to end the war, a sentiment held by Hattie's little girl, Nellie, who proudly stated, "He can do it, he knows everything."

January 22, 1918

Azelia, just recovering from pneumonia, "did some good work on the Mt. Raymond picture." She penned a newsy letter to Bob, and on the same day she wrote Willie and Ada, thanking them for the $10 money order they were always faithful in sending her.

In the Army, with the harsh Wawona winters and their seclusion behind him, and with care of his mother provided, Bob's career and personality opened like a flower in the sun. He learned heliography and the continental code and was delighted with everything and everyone at the camp in Monterey. The captain once approached him to ask what he thought of the organization, to which the young private replied that he loved everybody from the captain to the last private. The captain, so pleased, then told him: "Young man, if there is ever anything I can do for you, don't fail to come ask me."

Ada was busy with her new baby, William Wallace II, but managed time to knit Bob socks. Hattie sent him a robe and her husband, James, went for a week's visit. Bob sent back word to his mother that she need not worry about him smoking or drinking for he would take care of himself. It was good that Azelia had a last comforting word from him.

James applauded him as a wonder, and once again Nellie spoke her own confidence in him. "When Bob gets over there, the war will stop because Bob Bruce knows everything and he will tell the Kaiser what he's got to do in a hurry!"

Even with the worry of her youngest behind her,

Albert Henry Bruce and James Albert Spelt.
(Roberta Bruce Phillips Collection.)

Azelia was pressed with another concern. The Melones Mine was being sued for encroaching upon another mining claim and trouble brewed. She feared someone would blow it up and was therefore anxious for Willie to get out of there.

It was the last time she had to worry. The letters were the last she would pen. Only a week later, on January 31, 1918, she died at Hattie's house from double pneumonia and asthma. All her cares were ended.

From his hospital bed, where he was confined with mumps for two weeks, Private Robert Bruce wrote Willie in early February. Now, seeing the old homestead through eyes other than those viewing it from the angle of hardship, his affection surfaced. He hoped that the estate would be administered in such a fashion that its sale would be forestalled, and that Jay would take a reasonable view in this direction. They had all worked so hard for it, he pleaded.

He was now at Camp Merritt, New Jersey, and the journey there had exulted him. The troops had spent 19 days at sea, sailing through the Panama Canal. With six hours shore leave, he and two others hired an auto and toured the city from one end to the other. The three visited plantations with tropical fruits growing upon them, and for once he had all the bananas he could eat. The bananas turned into something of a caper for him. He brought 15 dozen aboard the ship and once out of sight of land, sold them to the sailors at 5 cents each. The excursion was thus paid for. After nine hours sailing through the canal, the transport sailed into the Caribbean Sea, whose reputation as a rough body of water was proved as "the ship danced a jig."

Bob was even more delighted with Camp Merritt than he had been at Monterey. It was a little city unto itself with a library, moving picture houses and fine accommodations kept warm, even with plenty of snow outside and the Wawona-like cold climate. With enthusiastic delight, he wrote Will and Ada: "The people on the Eastern coast are certainly war conscious. Every town we passed through we were cheered, nothing seems too good for a soldier in N. J. All the high class places are open to us, and they even allow us to go in some of the theaters without payment, so patriotic are the people feeling."

He had toiled in the mines, worked at Wawona in situations as varying as waiting table to fitting pipes to the swimming pool. He had never gone East until now, but at last had found his niche.

By March, 1918, he was with the American Expeditionary Force in France, and his regard for Uncle Sam was unimpaired, as he considered himself well-situated with everything needed for his comfort. The circumstances of his fighting in France aside, he loved the country and appreciated the people's high regard for both Americans and all things American. He loved both the little farms and wide boulevards of Paris. After a trip to the palace of Louis XIV at Versailles, he expressed little doubt that the French had earned the reputation as being the most artistic people in the world.

On the sober side, he met many Belgians who had lost their country to the Germans. "If all the Americans could hear what they have to tell they would certainly empty their purses to buy Liberty Bonds," he wrote Jeanette.

He saw Paris, the city which was transformed from "The city of light" to "The city of night," as one of its citizens described his revered city to the young American. And then Bob saw the trenches. A letter to Hattie told it like it was:

American Expeditionary Forces
Oct. 24th, 1918
Dear Sister

I am well contented and have everything I need for my comfort so never worry about me. . . . About sending a Christmas gift. . . . I would rather you would give the money to the Red Cross and don't forget the Salvation Army as they are both doing great work over here. We have certainly been working plenty during these last offensives and we have been under shell fire considerable and we have three casualties as the result. I saw several fellows wounded, one group of soldiers were all cut up when standing only 75 feet away. Another time a shell came over our heads and landed about 30 feet away, but it was a dud (a dud is a shell which fails to explode) or I shouldn't be writing this letter. These artillery shells certainly do wicked execution when they burst and scatter shrapnel about and I certainly am glad to be in the rear once again, not that I was much afraid, one always seems to think he is not the one who is going to get it. . . . The great objection is the living conditions being so bad, for about a month we lived in dugouts and say, you should see the rats in these places. They will actually carry your clothes away at night, that is, if you are not sleeping in them, which you most always are. I didn't have mine off for more than two weeks. Of course, the whole conversation now is the front and we have many discussions about whether you see the shell explode before you hear the whistle or whether you hear it whistle before the explosion. The whole question depends on the velocity of the shell and of the sound it makes. . . .

Well, I am surprised at the inefficiency of modern war. So much material is used to accomplish such small results. Dozen of shells fall which do no damage whatsoever, no wonder it cost them thousands of dollars to kill a man with modern machinery, when Julius Caesar could kill all he wanted to at the rate of fifty cents a head. . . .

There is every indication the war will be over before many more months. Of course, winter is almost here now and winter is the best ally the Huns have, so I do not expect the war to finish until next year, but feel we must do a good job while we are about it. The war has demonstrated many things to my mind and one thing especially is that the U. S. is the greatest nation in the universe. We are all thrilled at the unprecedented way America is building ships, factories and massing the material with which to crush the Huns.

Even in the trenches, Bob's scientific mind was inquiring as he asked Hattie to have James contact Prof. Larkin and ask, "What is the velocity of the shells now in use on the Western Front and also what is the velocity of sound and if the velocity of sound is effected by temperature."

On November 11, 1918, he left the mud, the rats, the trenches and the bursting shells behind.

Out of the Army, he went to work for the Mountain King Mine, earning $4.50 per day.

The sun seemed to shine on Bob's post-war life and employment. By the first of September 1923, he returned to the Hotel Whitcomb in San Francisco, where he had earlier worked. He had left his position there the previous spring, but concurrent with his arrival in the City, the man who filled the position quit, and Bob got back his job as assistant engineer. He was grateful to the Lord for the goodness he now enjoyed, he wrote his Wawona kin, among them Bill, who was there once again. "When you come down, will you bring my fiddle?" he asked.

But the sun also set. It was at the Whitcomb on March 1, 1924. Bob was on top of the elevator cage at the sixth level, repairing the door, and when he gave the signal to descend, Olympia Mazo, the operator inside the elevator, complied. It was not until the second landing that the operator noticed blood dripping into the elevator. Bob was found on top of the cage, his skull crushed by the counter weight of the elevator. It was ten o'clock that morning when the fiddle was forever stilled. He was twenty-nine years old.

15 The Cougar Hunter

One of life's inevitable setbacks nailed Jay Cook Bruce, but ultimately opened wide the door to the career which shaped the rest of his life. He had designed and built a water-powered sawmill at Redding, California, and his new business thrived as the mill turned out lumber. But then he was laid low with blood poisoning in his left hand, which left him perilously close to death. This was 1915, with no cure on the horizon. To his sorrow, he learned just how unscrupulous was his partner. During this period of terrible agony, he was unable to fulfill the lumber contracts, so the partner sued him. Through the decision of the court, the partner won the case.

Jay lost not only the sawmill, but his home, and was left with a crippled hand.

At this time, cougars ran the mountains rampantly and were considered unacceptable predators by both ranchers and farmers. The County offered a bounty of $20 for killing a male cougar and raised it $5 for a female. In some southern counties, the bounty went as high as $50 to $60. With this in mind, but more to get her depressed husband outside again, Katherine suggested he go hunting.

For this new line of work, he needed cougar trackers, and rounded up several hunting dogs. With his dogs, Jay drove his car as close as the terrain would allow and then let the dogs do their thing. They howled on a certain treble when they spotted the cougar, and the rest was up to the hunter.

Jay and trackers quickly came to the attention of California's Fish and Game Commission, who thought he just might be the answer to an ongoing problem they were dealing with. Ranchers were bitterly complaining of the hundreds of head of cattle and goats they were losing to this predator, the mountain lion.

In 1918, the Commission and Jay struck a deal and he became the first State Mountain Lion Hunter. He would work throughout the state for $25 per week and also be allowed, at his insistence, to collect bounty and sell the pelts. This career, easily extended from his mountain days of hunting, opened doors to aspects of his life and character that perhaps even he did not realize were lurking underneath his skin. He became quite a showman, successful author and spellbinding storyteller, as stories of his hunts unfolded in various forms.

Hunting swept the calendar. Only snow or rain kept the hunter in. Jay tried to conduct his hunting in areas where abandoned cabins could offer him shelter in a storm. During any such storm, he spent his time writing articles about his experiences, selling them to *Field and Stream* and *Outdoor Life* magazines.

Enter the Snows. It was 1923. Henry Snow, with his cameraman son, Sidney, had embarked on a three-year African safari. Henry hunted while Sidney rolled the camera. The result was a movie titled *Hunting Big Game in Africa with Guns and Camera*. It was only natural that the duo teamed up with California's prime mountain lion hunter to make another movie. Jay, already half showman, was ready to perform.

Some who knew Jay wryly proclaimed that if any Hollywood studio tried to transform him into a handsome movie hero, it would fail miserably. He was a thin, wiry man, often sporting a scraggly beard. He possessed boundless energy and spirit and also a sense of humor. After the Hollywood crowd had failed to turn him into a nattily-dressed superhero, he observed of himself: "I ask you, what good would silk socks and plucked eyebrows do when I come up against one of those birds? Why, if I let them movie directors make me pretty, the doggone cougar might turn around and undo all their work!"

The Snows contented themselves with the film's climax where Jay lassoed a 160-pound cougar.

The movie was a hit, and Jay took to the road, as actors did in pre-television days, to promote the movie and entertain the audience with personal appearances on the stage. He also spoke to service clubs in New York, Chicago, Boston and many other cities. He loved this. He loved the appreciative audiences and he loved his own brand of entertainment. New Yorkers could be somewhat jaded, having seen animal acts with bears and dogs on stage, but when Jay shared the spotlight with his cougar, a thrill of fear and excitement swept through the audience. Scenes from his own tracking experiences might well have made their best movie for him and the Snows.

In January of 1924, Jay was sent on a hunting expedition to an area adjoining the western boundary of General Grant National Park in Fresno County. There the mountain lions were accused of decimating the deer population. He tracked more than the lion. In that wilderness of brush, trees, and in January-deep snow, he flushed out a moonshiner pretending to be a miner, who was catering to the high school crowd, as it was later discovered.

His next catch was three scruffily dressed youths beside a battered Model T Ford and a stack of fishing rods, rifles, shotguns and camping equipment, all suspiciously shining with newness. Immediately, he sensed something was not right, at the same time realizing he was in a situation where extricating himself would require a careful defusing lest he be shot in the back. His old tracking skill kicked in, and on impulse, he offered to show the three youths lion tracks on the road a few yards away. It was his good luck the tracks were there, left only two nights previously, he told the kids. It diverted their attention long enough for him to safely make haste.

From the nearest ranger station, the sheriff was contacted, and in a short time, the three were surprised at their camp and arrested for the robbing of a hardware and sporting goods store in Fresno only a few nights before.

Over a three-year period, he and Jay Jr., then fifteen, filmed their own action movie. Jay Jr. was the cameraman. It was during this venture that another disaster struck at Jay. His hounds had caught cougar-scent and the two filmmakers struggled through the thick underbrush on the trail of these stars of the film. A sharp twig snagged the elder Bruce's eye, blinding him instantly. Suffering terribly, he was guided back to his car by his son. He was to lose sight permanently in that eye.

The two movies the Snows made helped make Jay a celebrity around the Mother Lode towns. Locals pointed him out to strangers as the area's most successful bounty hunter. He was their own.

A bureaucratic glitch very nearly undid his career with the state when that body hired several more hunters. Now, a Civil Service examination was given, and Jay, answering from his wide experience in the field and in the mountains, rather than from the text, failed the test. He protested that both questions and answers were based on storybook knowledge and, surprisingly, state officials then asked him to write the examination. He did, took the test once more and passed.

After 28 years his marriage to Katherine ended in 1938. Their range of different interests was too great. Jay then married Grace Campbell, a musician who had played oboe with the Boston Fayettes, an all-girl band.

On August 12, 1940, Jay wrote to his sister, Jeanette, now Mrs. Colburn:

I have just bought 20 acres with ¼ mile of a trout stream containing water enough to supply a trout farm, irrigation, power for a hundred lights with 200 feet of pipe line. I have already started a lodge of stone and logs, but can only work on it at odd times or hire $30 per month in work. It is on the north rim of the South Fork of the American River at elevation of 2000 feet, heavily timbered with Douglas fir, yellow pine, black oak, live oak and cedar.

He was clearly enthralled with the place.

There on the picturesque stream he established the Bear Creek Musical Center. A versatile musician gifted on the mandolin, violin, banjo, guitar and some piano chords, Jay's passion for the sweet notes of music soon drew many musicians to the home for happy hours of playing.

He once wrote that he had been forced into the lion hunting business to keep his family from going hungry. Once in the business, he gave it all he had "starting a program, which developed into a comprehensive program of predatory animal control and increased our deer supply seven fold over a period of 30 years."

After 30 years of service with the Fish and Game Commission, he retired. In this time he had killed 669 mountain lions, 40 bears and hundreds of rattlesnakes, as well as snagging a few outlaws. He was satisfied with the way his career had progressed, and in his retirement he could write the book that had been on his mind for years. In 1953, his *Cougar Killer* became a best seller.

Written with insight and descriptive power, the book brought him a nomination to honorary membership in the "Mark Twain International Society." This was a prestigious society with Mark Twain's cousin, Cyril Clemens as president. On the honorary membership list were such luminaries as Dwight Eisenhower, Winston Churchill and Ernest Hemingway. Jay was keeping excellent company.

He was always eager to give Grace credit and praise for the long hours she spent editing and rewriting his book for him, and he appreciated her own accomplishments.

Of his four children by Katherine:

Jay Jr. is coining money in a radio and television shop he has in Hayward; Wilson is working as a cannery inspector for the State Board of Health and earning a good salary. Elizabeth and her husband, George Brown moved to Reno with their three children. George was on the airplane carrier, Lexington, when the Japs dive-bombed it, and got a Presidential citation for his part in it, the possibility of an A-bomb attack on the Bay Area scared him into selling their home in Hayward and moving to Reno.

He gave Jeanette a microscopic view of his brood. And daughter Katherine and her husband had just met them at the post office where they "went to have a turkey sent to them."

That afternoon Jay and Grace cooked the turkey for their Christmas dinner.

16 Camp Chilnualna

CAMP CHILNUALNA
OVER THE BRIDGE AT WAWONA

Adjoining Yosemite Valley, the Big Trees,
Glacier Point, Signal Peak.
Fine hunting and fishing, scenery and climate
and plenty of pure water.
Best camping grounds and fine swimming.
Furnished cottages for housekeeping.
Only 2 hours drive to Yosemite Valley.
Home cooking. Lunches 60¢; Meals $1.00.
Comfortable clean beds, $1.00.
Furnished cottages for housekeeping
from $20 per month.

This advertisement told the story,
as did this second one:

OWN A SUMMER HOME

Own a beautiful wooded lot at Chilnualna Villa,
near the popular summer resort of Wawona, on
Chilnualna Falls Drive, on the north bank of the
South Fork of the Merced River, adjoining
Yosemite National Park. Fine hunting and fishing,
wonderful scenery and climate, plenty of
pure water. Large lots from $100 up.
Summer cottages built to order. Lumber at rates.
Only a limited number of lots for sale; get yours
quick. A few hours by auto from San Joaquin
valley points.
Four thousand feet elevation. The Big Trees,
Yosemite Valley, Glacier Point, Signal Peak
and numerous points of interest are within
short auto drives.
Chilnualna Falls on the grounds.
Apply A. W. Spelt, Owner and Builder
Care of Bruce Brothers,
Wawona, Mariposa Co., Calif.

It had become clear that Wawona was growing
up, filling up, expanding with people where only
the pines had stood before. The Chilnualna Cabins
helped bring in the tourists.

A. W. Spelt was proud and happy to advertise

his new cottages. After Azelia's property was divided in 1919, Hattie gave a six-acre parcel to her father-in-law, Albert Spelt. In 1920, he began building small, slab-sided cabins, using waste material in the form of slabs from the Bruce Sawmill. Slabs are the rounded bark part of the tree, which are cut off to get to the prime lumber of the tree.

The six cabins were named Fir, Cedar, Oak, Laurel, Daisy, and Pine Cone. Pine Cone was the main house where the Spelts lived and managed the operation. Its life began as a tent, with wooden walls and a roof eventually added.

Albert Spelt and his family left San Francisco for Wawona in March to ready the cabins and tents of Camp Chilnualna. A family with boys was hired, the idea being that the boys could work in the

Pantomime or charades, whichever, cousins Albert O. Bruce and Nellie Spelt seem to be in tune with one another. *(Morrie Bruce Collection.)*

Camp Chilnualna lured the city-bound. Nellie Spelt riding Malcolm Fulmer's horse. *(Malcolm Fulmer Collection.)*

extensive garden Albert Spelt had planted in strawberries and vegetables for the restaurant. The boys were not necessarily crazy about gardening, but the mother and daughter of this hired family baked breads and cakes. Orders were taken from all over Wawona.

The largest room of the "White House," built in 1892 and intended for a school, was used as the restaurant. Hattie and James' daughter, Nellie, found it quite interesting to work there when she was twelve and thirteen.

"Chester Riles from the Fresno paper and Mary Baker Eddy from the churches, all these people stayed the summer there," Wally Bruce was to recall.

In 1926, Albert Spelt traded his holdings to Cornelia McBeth Wooster for an apartment complex in Oakland. She added the Manzanita, and in 1936, sold Camp Chilnualna to Harold May for $6,500. He operated the camp until his death when it was passed on to his son, Norman. Norman and his wife, Patricia, ran the camp until they retired. Camp Chilnualna is presently managed by "Redwoods."

Hauling lumber to build Camp Chilnualna, 1920. Homestead House in the background. *(Roberta Bruce Phillips Collection.)*

17 The Return

Sam Harris was the son of James Marshall Harris, who raised fruits and vegetables on his land on the west side of Chowchilla Mountain. James Harris crossed the mountain to peddle his produce in Wawona. Thus it was that a young Sam made the acquaintance of a young Hattie Bruce, who was still living on the homestead in Chilnualna Park.

One day in San Francisco, years down the track, Hattie Spelt showed an apartment she had for rent to an inquiring man with two daughters. It happened to be Sam, who she did not recognize. Sam had a tic in one eye and Hattie thought he was winking at her. This made her a little nervous until Sam identified himself.

Hattie and James Spelt divorced, and after a stroke ended her Western Union career, Hattie returned to Wawona. She began working as a cook for her cousin, Charles Higgins, at nearby Breuner Meadows. It was when Sam was called to Bruener Meadows to do some carpentry work that he and Hattie renewed their acquaintance.

Sam earned a reputation that outlived him. He could do anything. He invented a shingle-making machine, which turned out shingles for the building industry. He turned his craft toward the skies when he began constructing an airplane. And on long sheets of paper he loved working in mathematics.

When he and Hattie married November 21, 1941, he built a large house on an upper plot of Section 35. It stands today.

Life back on her land was not always tranquil for Hattie. Aggravated by the increasing number of tourists, who made their way over her property for a look at Chilnualna Falls, she hauled out her chain saw and felled some pines across the path. When the steady intrusion called for more stringent deterrents, she parked herself below the falls with her shotgun across her lap.

Hattie Harris shows her indomitable fortitude at Bruener Meadows in 1942. The apple crop was good that year. *(Roberta Bruce Phillips Collection.)*

Sam Harris. Fate and geography brought Hattie Bruce Spelt and Sam Harris together after two daughters each (with their first spouses) and several years.
(Roberta Bruce Phillips Collection.)

There were peaceful, enjoyable times. Often, when she wasn't felling the obstructive trees, she went up the trail with her Bible and a book of poems, found a comfortable niche and communed with the grandeur of her special paradise.

Hattie was a keeper of the flame, historian, protector of her heritage and property and committed to setting facts straight. She wrote, extolled, beseeched, profaned, chastised and honored with a million words. She was vocal, argumentative, dedicated and supportive of those who deserved this honor, and chagrin with those who did not. She became a well-known critic of Park Service policies and became an avid letter writer, informing congressmen, senators and park management of their shortcomings. Yet she was often called upon to remember, and in one letter to Park Naturalist Douglass Hubbard, she recalled an incident between her mother and John Washburn.

"John was always jealous of our ownership of Chilnualna Falls. He would call them 'his falls.'"

One year the Washburns were hosting Governor Hill of New York and his large party. All the men bedded down in the barn, but sleeping quarters were still in short supply. John Washburn then went to the Bruces with an amazing story. To Azelia, he insisted, ". . . Charles Leidig and I have been going over the surveys in here and find the line way East, so that house you built for a school is on our property and I want the key. . . ."

Azelia remained unperturbed, quick to mention the government surveyor she had hired from the Land Office, and further informed John that he might lose his wagon shop, blacksmith shop, harness shop and the Hill's Studio, as well as the loading platform in front of the Hotel—if he were so insistent as to talk about surveys and stakes. In light of this run-down of the components of his empire, John Washburn backed down with a "Phsaw, Azelia, I better get Leidig and move the stakes back."

The conversation took on an even livelier tone when Azelia replied that was so or he'd face the Federal penitentiary, as it was a crime to move stakes. She was then gracious enough to rent her building for ten dollars, and an appeasement of sorts was made. Whether or not the stakes had been juggled, no one could say for sure.

Although Hattie's estimation could have been exaggerated, it certainly came from her heart and sincere inner beliefs when she proclaimed: "With the coming of the Army, came the most brutal force of government."

Clearly, she felt, "It was us against them."

Her conviction could either have been born or borne out by an encounter her mother once had with a Cavalry officer. A gold-bedecked Captain Benson rode up on the homestead one early morning and was greeted by Azelia, who offered him her hospitality. The captain declined, stating his mission. "I just want to find out how these Washburn brothers acquired all this land. Mrs. Bruce, you

have been a long time in these hills and you must know."

Azelia gave him a long and penetrating look before answering, "Captain Benson, there is just one piece of land in these hills in which I am interested and it is this piece of land, and if my title is ever attacked I shall defend it as my forefathers defended this great nation, by arms if necessary. There will be another Molly Pitcher in these hills!"

Captain Benson was speedy in his protest. "Mrs. Bruce, we do not intend to attack your title." Then, thinking he might have overstepped future policy, he qualified, "Not for the present at least."

Azelia shot him a look full of daggers. He tossed the reins over his horse's head and rode away, muttering, "I believe that woman would shoot." He had given her a fair estimation!

Hattie once wrote a Yosemite superintendent that she saw the Army as a policing force which "Curtailed the freedom of man." She recalled one event from the Cavalry days, never relenting in her great disdain.

A Cavalry patrol rode down from the high country and through the Bruce yard. There the troops halted, untied their tin cups from their saddles and drank from the water barrel. Three sheepherders, just expelled from the park, walked behind the horses, and one was obviously injured. His arm was in a sling made from part of his own shirt, the rest of his shirt wrapped around a head wound "administered by the forces of law and order."

The herders' dogs had been shot, their rifles broken, and their herds scattered.

Little sister, Jeanie, ran out and offered cups of water to the unfortunate herders, but the cup was struck from her hand by a patrolman, with a stern admonition. "These men are prisoners." Jeanie stamped her foot and, picking up the cup, did her own admonishing. "They are thirsty, too!" And she gave the herders water while the captors looked on in amazement.

One of the grateful sheepherders reached into his pocket and pulled out a "Widow's Mite," the Lord's prayer engraved upon it, and handed this treasure of his to the little benefactor. "Little girl, take this and the Lord bless you for all the days of your life, believe in God and always be good."

On one occasion, as told by Hattie years down

the track, politics and policy cut a cruel swath through piety.

Robert Wellman, with his sister, Eunice, trekked into the Wawona area to establish a Homestead. The two were no relation to the resident Bruces, but the children, out of affection, called them Uncle Bob and Aunty Eunice. Uncle Bob was an agnostic, but his sister was a True Believer, and shortly took over the religious education of the Bruce children. The way she espoused the dogma, all should be washed white in the blood of the lamb, a picture Azelia didn't favor for her children. Too literal for young minds. So Eunice took a different approach to her teachings, telling them of Joseph and his many-colored coat. This was such a splendid picture for the children to relate to that they began saving all scraps and made themselves bright jackets during the winter months.

Eunice and Robert claimed on a section about 12 or 14 miles higher in the mountains, reached by a narrow trail defined only by sheep having been driven over it to pasture. Robert drove his cattle up from the Elkhorn Ranch, he and his sister on horseback. This rough trip so tired Eunice that she stayed with the Bruces while Bob took the cattle up the narrowly defined trail. The gentle Eunice and affectionate Bob became part of their adopted family, and the children loved them.

The Homestead Law required that for six months the land had to be occupied, and that, strictly defined, meant it had to be slept on every night of those six months. The hopefuls arrived in May with the melting of snow in the upper ranges and stayed until the fall's snow drove them back to Hornitos and the ranch.

Aunty Eunice was deathly afraid of the bears. Old timer, Jim Duncan, had killed 80 of them already, and the number cemented in Eunice's mind, she did not trust God's protection against bears. When supplies were needed, Bob took Eunice to stay under the Bruces' protection, while he rode out for their necessities, and thus they missed a required night's residency on their land.

When it was time to go to the U. S. Land Office, they both dressed in their best, saddled the horses and rode with the certainty that their cherished land would soon be officially theirs.

The Land Office officer tackled Eunice first, told her to put her hand on the Bible and reminded her

"To tell the truth and nothing but the truth, so help me God." His first question was the fateful one. "Did you sleep upon the land every night for six months of the year?"

It was said that Eunice shook as she gave him her reply. "I cannot swear to that in the sight of God with my hand on his word."

The title was denied.

Bob returned to Wawona a broken and destroyed man. "Azelia Bruce, had there been a living God, he would have risen in protest" he told Azelia with dejection.

The cattle were driven back to the Elkhorn.

An old man returned in 1928 to show some of the Bruce children his promised land and to take one last look at it before he passed out of sight forever. The old mule, Fanny, neighed with recognition when she hit that sheep-broken trail. Up at his promised land, Uncle Bob called attention to the beauties of God's creation for man, which the government had denied him.

When Hattie was a venerable eighty-one, word came to her through her son-in-law, Lester Phillips, that Karl M. Kidder of the *Fresno Bee* "Would like an interview with that old woman known as Harriet Bruce Harris." Hattie seemed to have taken no exception to what she might well have considered careless phrasing of her aged condition, and answered his query in a letter informing him of what she had done in her lifetime, plus a lot of what she thought.

> I have helped drill holes to blast boulders, built rock walls, cut wood, both sawed and split, leveled land, plowed, planted orchards, milked cows, raised strawberries, split shingle blocks and helped on the shingle mill baling and counting shingles, dug trench and laid thousands of feet of pipe, digging four-hundred foot trench in one day, worked 36 years for the Western Union and never made but one error that cost the company anything, and that was a minor one. I raised two daughters and put them through school. I raised chickens and sold eggs, sewed dresses, washed windows, papered walls, read and studied Shakespeare, Pope, Byron, Moore, and many others.

And then she went on to declare part of her philosophy. "I believe in government that builds a sound financial policy, not leaving the coming generation to meet our bills that we may have prosperity now." Right on, Hattie!

Mr. Kidder, reading Hattie's letter, was surely given a fair appraisal of just who she was.

Her regard and estimation of people within her association was variable. Some she held in low esteem and some were marginal, but of the Washburns, there is no doubt of her high regard.

For the National Park Service and posterity, Hattie set down some stories of area pioneers. The Jim Lawrence story is part of Wawona history, and says something of the evolution of the times. Jim Lawrence shot Bushhead Tom, and according to Hattie's account, that act was justifiable. Bushhead Tom, an Indian, "had beaten the squaws, beaten Jim's daughter, wife to Archie Leonard, and was on his way to kill all white babies. His mission that day of the killing was to beat the brains out of Clarence Washburn against the store porch post. Jim Lawrence rested the gun on that same post and shot Bushhead Tom as he came over the hill near the bear pen."

When the case went to trial, Jim Lawrence was acquitted.

Jim Lawrence should have had a ballad written about him . . . if all he said of himself was true. He had lost the first joint on his index finger and loved holding up the stub to an enthralled audience to whom he told the story. He had lost it during the Civil War, where he was a bushwhacker, always on the side with the most and best whiskey barrels. He was invariably asked, "Was it shot off?" His reply was always quick, always consistent. "No better cause than the Civil War. They put the whiskey barrel on two logs and when they turned the spigot on, it broke. I stuck my finger into the hole to save the whiskey and by the time they repaired the spigot it swelled and I could not pull it out, so they just cut it off and I pulled it out and they drove the end out tight with the new spigot. By golly, it was a good cause." Of course.

Nathan B. (Pike) Phillips was an early guide in the area. In 1961, Hattie wrote to Park Naturalist Douglass Hubbard, something of what she remembered of the old man her family had loved. He taught Bert violin, Bert playing by ear until his mother taught him the notes. When Pike's last illness grounded him, Hattie stayed long hours by his side, tending him until she gave herself away by fainting in school from fatigue. Pike was then moved to a room over the store where a porter cared for him. When he died, Gus Wintermute made his coffin and John Washburn furnished one of his own suits for burial.

Hattie's stroke might have stilled her hands with the telegrapher keys, but her pen never ran dry. Back on the homestead land with Sam, she determined to admonish on points she deemed incorrect in her admitted effort to set her history straight.

She had her own ideas on conservation, which she was intent on sharing with Congressman Harold (Bizz) Johnson. She felt the sheepmen and cattlemen had aided the park with their animals clearing the dense underbrush and dry grass, often prone to fire. In a time when the practice was neither favored nor adopted, she prescribed burning this underbrush. "Today we need a cleaning out of these forests and useless underbrush to leave the water free for the use of growth of young trees. The place is a mess."

In his autobiographical book, *Cougar Killer*, her brother, Jay, wrote of trying, though unsuccessfully, to convince the foresters that the jungle of forest entanglements should be burned.

Interestingly, Yosemite forester Emil Ernst campaigned to have this burning as the resident Indians had always done, but he, too, was unsuccessful in his many attempts. It was to take several more years before the practice was adopted.

Hattie once wrote to Senator Thomas H. Kuchel: "My hands are almost useless, but my voice is loud and may prove a support to free government and preservation of the Constitution."

It can be said that Hattie was always active in communication.

18 Recollections

On Armistice Day 1935 Charlotte Bruce Gibner penned a memoir. It was of another time, another place, and it was done with a poignancy that her memories evoked. Her own special time began on May 19, 1880.

Her father was Johnny Bridle Bruce, partner in the Big Tree Station complex, and she first went to the Station at three weeks old. She was born in Merced where there was a doctor, her father staying with the business. Johnny had his heart set on a boy, because in his family, each alternate generation had a John Bruce and then a Charles Bruce. He already had two daughters and no idea what this last baby would be until the stage landed at the platform in front of the Hotel and his daughter, Fannie, cried out: "Oh, Daddy, it's a girl and it's a redhead." So he had to be satisfied with a Charlotte instead of a Charles.

Charlotte wrote:

This might be called the Periclean Age of Wawona and Yosemite, because here was a civilization second to none. The stages were running and a most select group of people came from over the world. I can remember a night at Wawona when the logs were blazing in the office and there was gathered there a United States Senator, stage drivers, Indian guides, an East Indian prince and various Army officers, and yet it seemed to be an amalgamated group. If the stage was late, fears were expressed that it was some new stage robbery, as was not uncommon in those times. If any notables were coming their names were posted on the bulletin board, and I remember going to see what was posted when later we children arrived. I was greeted by this notice posted in a prominent place: H. A. Washburn, 5 kids and a box of dogs.

On the old stage road, you didn't see the Valley, nor did you get even a glimpse of it until you struck Inspiration Point, where you saw it all at once. It was such a breathtaking sight that many people burst into tears.

Wawona was famous for its food. It had its own garden from which all the vegetables came; they killed their own meat; they fished out of the rivers. Milk came from their own herd of cows and in game season there was quail on toast and venison. A typical Wawona breakfast consisted of fruit in season, beefsteak, ham and eggs, trout, hot cakes and cornbread with homemade preserves. This was not to give the diner a choice, but to be eaten in its entirety. The rate for room and board was $4 per day.

During the regime from 1880 to 1905, the Valley and Wawona were governed first by a commissioner from the State of California. They made an annual trip, accompanied by much fanfare, to inspect the Valley and create the laws by which the Valley was run. Then came the establishment of Yosemite National Park and the Army was called upon to keep out the sheep and stock the streams, and a fish hatchery was established at Wawona. . . .

President Theodore Roosevelt made the tour to Yosemite and I was present when he was greeted at a champagne luncheon by the Washburns at the Big Trees. I have the picture of President Roosevelt and Galen Clark riding through the Valley.

Henry Washburn and J. J. Cook were the leading spirits of the Valley, and they were greatly assisted by their two beautiful wives, Jean Bruce Washburn and Fannie Bruce Cook. These ladies came from an old Scottish family and had both talent and personality and did much to make Wawona a delightful place both to visit and to live in.

John Bruce, their nephew, was associated with Henry Washburn and J. J. Cook, and he too, became so enamored of the Valley that he spent all the money he made in Mariposa to keep Wawona going.

Henry Washburn was a great leader of men. Of the hundred or more men whom he employed, there was not one who wouldn't have risked his life for him. I remember the great fires in the Big Trees year after year, when he and his men worked night and day digging trenches around them to save them. . . .

He always saw that those who worked for him were well fed and that the food was the best. The children of the workers were always well cared for in sickness and in health. The first offer of employment always went to the people of the town of Mariposa, as he felt it his duty to care for those who surrounded him. He was the most benevolent man I ever knew.

His chief interest was the Valley. He was always building new roads, one of which was the Dewey Trail, which branched out all over the Valley on the Glacier Point side. He put out bids for building this trail, but the price was exorbitant, so he went to one of the old-timers, one John Conway, an old pioneer, and asked him what he could do it for. Conway said, "Well, Henry, if they say they can build that trail for $10,000, I can build it for $300." Henry said, "Go ahead, Conway." Conway thereupon got 30 horses and mules and let them pick their own way along, thus insuring the easiest grades and the firmest ground. Driving the horses and mules back and forth over this path then packed the ground firmly, and the Dewey Trail was born.

A child was always welcome in Henry Washburn's sight, and at dinner time in his hotels, you could always see the children of those who worked for him standing around with pitchers and bowls ready to take home the ice cream they knew would be forthcoming. He was also the friend of the Indians, and supplied them with food, as well as taking a great interest in the Indian camps in the Valley. He was a man who could walk with the mightiest or the most humble, as he had the common human touch.

Yosemite Valley owes much of its preservation to him, as he was never known to cut down a tree for mercenary reasons. He became an ardent Californian, and no native son could equal him in that respect. Little by little he brought nearly half the town of Putney to Mariposa and the Valley.

The Wawona Hotel, of which he was part owner, was in his day a hostelry second to none, and famous for its food. The head cook, Ah You, was there for 47 years and had five Chinese under him. His cooking was so excellent that many of the guests, including Seward Webb, an Easterner of some repute as a gourmet, asked to see the cook who could put forth such pastries. . . .

The day came, however, when it was said that they would have to retrench at Wawona, and it was decided to let some of the old timers go. Most of them were able to find work elsewhere, but one old fellow said, "Henry, I have been here 25 years and you are not going to send me away now. I am going to live and die here." Henry put him back to work.

Charlotte's father died when she was only two, her mother a mere five years later, at which time her great aunt and great uncle assumed the raising of her and her two sisters. Henry Washburn was, doubtlessly, her father figure, as well as friend and generous provider.

Allen Kilgour had left his wife, Jeanette, with the upbringing of their four children in 1914, and the children lost track of him.

His granddaughter, Hope Higbee, recalled excursions that she and her mother, Hester Stephan made on many Sunday afternoons during World War II. They were looking for Allen, the handsome trooper who long before had won Jeanette's heart.

For years Hester talked about finding her father, and checked out many leads. Finally, she did get information from the Spanish-American War, and she and Hope drove to San Leandro where they suspected Allen might be living. When Hester attempted to pinpoint the house, Hope, with an uncanny instinct, said, "No, not that house." Hester laughed, asking, "How do you know?" To which Hope could only say, "I just can tell. It's not that house."

The two drove along until Hope pointed to a house with a beautiful yard. "That's where grandpa lives," she told her mother. "How do you know?" Hester was curious. "I don't know, but the yard is beautiful."

Hester pulled the car over, and that's where her father lived. The pair knocked on the door, and when a lady answered, Hester told her she was looking for Allen Kilgour. The lady replied, "Well, there is no Allen Kilgour here. There is a Mr. Dugger. Mr. Richard Dugger."

A disappointed Hester admitted they had made

a mistake and was poised to leave when the lady surprised her by suddenly admitting that Hester had not made a mistake and invited the two in. She then called to her husband.

When Richard Dugger saw the two, he cried out, "Oh my God, oh my God, Jeanette." For a moment he thought that Hester was Jeanette, his ex-wife, and that Hope was Hester, his daughter.

Hope recalled: "He started to cry and he got really upset. He just grabbed us and kissed us. He asked, 'How did you find me?' and Mama said, 'Well, it's taken me 32 years.'"

Allen had changed his name, though not legally. He took the name of a man with whom he had worked, a logger who was killed in a logging accident. He assumed the man's identity. He then went to work for the Southern Pacific Railroad, a well-paying job that helped put his new wife's seven children through college. He and his second wife had one son, Richard.

Hope spoke of her grandmother to her newly discovered uncle and his wife, Tina. Jeanette was a spiritualist minister with a church on Fell Street in San Francisco. "During the war, people would come to her saying they had received this terrible telegram and she would say, 'No, no, no, you go right back home, you're going to get a phone call that your son is o.k.,' and then, 'I know this.' And then people would come back the next day and pour money all over her, just handed her money like crazy, if it was true. In some cases it wasn't true, but in some cases she would invite them in and say, 'Well, you have to accept this.' She was very, very, very good."

Richard did not become an Instant Believer. "No way," he protested the idea that Jeanette could have any such power. But Tina became interested and planned a visit. "I'm going to make an appointment with your grandmother and I bet she'll never know who I am." Hope was quick to reply. "Oh, I think she will!"

The plan was for Tina to say she was a friend of a friend, name supplied by Hope. Hope and her Uncle Bob then drove Tina to within two blocks of 377 Fell Street. She walked up to the front stairs. It was when Jeanette opened the door that the plan fell apart. "I'm Tina. I'm here for my appointment."

"Oh no, you're not," Jeanette contradicted. "You know Allen Kilgour, you're related to that s.o.b.

Jeanette Bruce Kilgour, on the right, ordained a minister at her Spiritualist Church in San Francisco. Her grandchildren Gloria and Danny look serious for the occasion. *(Maddalena Gartin Collection.)*

somehow. You're not getting into my house. Where is that s.o.b.?" She ranted and raved at Tina, who could only say, when she finally ran back to the car and safety, "I believe, I believe!"

Jeanette's house on Fell Street had a basement, main floor and several upstairs rooms. The three levels afforded vastly different functions. She rented the upstairs rooms to single working men and lived in the main floor section. The basement was the special place. It was converted to a church where Jeanette conducted her Spiritual Ministry. During her regular Sunday evening meetings, the lights would be dimmed and a floor lamp with a fringed shade and red globe, standing by Jeanette's chair, would be lit.

She then went into a trance and summoned the spirits. Guests put some personal items into a basket passed around, and while in the trance, Jeanette gave a brief reading for each. After a sermon, an offering was received from the congregation.

Thursday afternoons were reserved for private meetings. These were held in the front room of her main floor living quarters. She had quite a following in San Francisco.

Jeanette often read the palms of her grandchildren. Everything came true.

Like her mother, Azelia, she was gifted in many ways. Before her ministries, she had been an excellent seamstress. She loved painting, being particularly fond of doing pansies on small canvases.

Wally Bruce remembered his aunt Jeanette, also. He and his family lived in San Francisco at the same time she conducted her ministry. He remembered her DeSoto as well as her reputation for being a good minister. "I drove around San Francisco with her and it took about five years of my life. She was a wild woman when she got behind the wheel of a car. She would go over those hills like a San Franciscan. She said she had a spinning wheel on the car. Every time she'd whip it around a turn, she let go of it, and, of course, it would naturally fly back to a straight course. She made you take a deep breath!"

In his fond recollections of his spirited aunts and uncles, Wally remembered his grandparents' library so well. As a kid in high school, he was captain of the debating team and loved to argue about most everything. In the homestead house library a book on speeches seemed to be a wonderful source of speeches and potential arguments, he hoped. He thumbed through the book, looking for Lincoln's Gettysburg Address, but the speech was missing. Now, what kind of book of speeches is this, he wondered, without Lincoln's Gettysburg Address in it? Upon closer inspection, he saw the book had been printed in 1858. Lincoln hadn't got around to delivering it yet.

His uncles were a sturdy bunch. "They would go out in the wintertime, when they were young pups and they'd go to work in the mines. My dad, sometimes he was a timberman, sometimes he'd be a hoist operator. And Bert would generally be a miner, so would Bob and Jay. Well, they'd go ahead and work in the mines until they got word that snow was leaving Wawona and they could open the sawmill. Then they would give notice at the mine and after they drew their pay on a Friday night, they'd take off, let's say from Nevada City or that

area, and hike for Wawona and never stop. They just kept going."

Wally spoke of Jay. "I can remember seeing Jay when I was a kid. Well, he was State Mountain Lion Hunter, and he would go out hunting lions. I'd see him take off from Wawona. He'd take a pack horse with him in case he was gonna have to stay over night. If he didn't, he would get back at five o'clock in the evening. He'd unpack the horse and the horse would lie down. He'd wash up, then he'd go on the hillside and have us throw cans and he'd practice shooting at the cans. And after he got tired of that, then he'd find someone around there to fight and he'd box for five or six rounds, then he'd have dinner and then he'd insist that the people went down to Camp Hoyle and he played dance music until two in the morning. He played the fiddle. He'd make my dad play mandolin and sometime trumpet for him."

Wally went on to describe his uncle. "Jay was pretty strong-willed. That is a complimentary way of saying that he was hard-headed."

Jay could make a kid nervous. He had returned once to Wawona to hunt and killed a mother lion who had two cubs. So he took the cubs and put them in a sack and brought them home. Now at that time he had a moving picture that he had developed along with Sid Snow, showing on how he hunted cougars. So he was going to take it over to the sawmill at Sugar Pine. He invited me to go along. Well, I was a little nervous about getting near him even, but I went along. As he changed the reels, he brought these two cubs out on the stage, gave me some leather gloves and says, 'Wally, go play with them cubs while I change the reels.' And that is how he acted generally."

Wally had a snake story or so, one in which he was a prime, though unsuspecting participant.

His father, Bill (Willie), was working for the Park Service in Yosemite when "Russell came down one day and said there was a funny odor up there and an odd noise and would you come up and take a look?" The older William Wallace agreed to take a look. The spot in question was where the creek comes down, with a sort of cavern underneath. He looked into that place, and there were about 500 rattlesnakes, twisted up and just coming awake. He got a couple sticks of dynamite, lit a fuse and threw it into the den, blowing the snakes all over the

Azelia's artistic genes were passed down to her son, William, as evidenced here. His brush strokes are under the guidance of artist Neil Sampson. *(W. Bruce Collection.)*

Wally and Bob had their ambitions. Bob planned to be a lawyer and prevailed upon the young Wally to also become one, and they would set up the firm of Bruce and Bruce. Together they would correct all of the injustices that had occurred in the United States up until that time. "Unfortunately, Bob was not able to get to that ambition and I didn't take up the law. I took up engineering and created more injustices than I corrected." Those comedian genes were passed down the line.

Of Hattie, Wally had a collection of memories. "Those who knew Hattie knew she was an exceptional person. I can remember going down to Merced with her one day. She went into the Western Union office and flashed her card, showing she was an operator. She hit that key and it just buzzed. And pretty soon the message came back, 'For Christ sake, Hattie, slow down!' Her touch had been recognized."

Hattie loved to fish. Back in the forties, when both she and Wally were in Wawona, they went out on opening day, usually Memorial Day. He recalled: "We'd go up fishing by the meadows by the campgrounds. It would be raining and the people would be in their tents, and we'd sneak by and get our limit of fish. Then we would keep one alive and come back and drop it in the creek right where all these guys were. Then we would fuss with it and catch it in front of them. These guys would run out with their fishing poles and whip that piece of creek to death, and then we brought the fish back with us. Hattie was the last of the generation, a mountain woman."

Hattie's career with Western Union might have ended with the stroke, but she was never outside the sphere of communication. One aspect ended while another began.

Wally went on to say, "I think that there were some politicians along the line that would have

country. "You know, for the next ten or 15 years, we never had a rattlesnake," Wally ended the story with what must have been some satisfaction.

Willie managed to get rid of another rattler, this one with a little more finesse. There were a lot of them around when Wally was a baby, and one day one of them crawled into Wally's cradle space where he lay sleeping under mosquito netting. Fortunate both that he was sleeping and the net offered somewhat of a deterrent to the snake's unauthorized cuddling. This potentially lethal situation was defused when Willie got his fishing pole and snagged the curled-up rattler.

Albert Olcott Bruce, Bert's boy, worked at the Rouse Mill. It was located on the south side of the Merced River by the Seventh Day Adventist Camp.
(Maddalena Gartin Collection.)

loved to see Aunt Hattie lose her pen or in some way calm her down. Because if you visit the *Mariposa Gazette* and Marguerite Campbell,[1] why she had a whole file full of letters Aunt Hattie had written her. And none of them were complimentary. Most of her congressmen had letters she had written and few of them were complimentary. If they had listened to her we probably would have had a better county in which to live."

In the days when the boys were running their sawmill, they would go out and fall and buck a tree before breakfast. They always carried a green bottle with kerosene in it and stuffed with pine needles. When the saw became sticky with pitch, the kerosene was poured on it to keep it free. Wally told a story on Bob. "Well, Dad and I went out one day and Bob was bucking a tree, just killing himself, jerking and pushing, and the saw was stuck in the log. Dad asked, 'Bob, why didn't you use your kerosene?' 'Aw, I forgot the damn stuff. Any damn fool who would come out here this late in the morning ought to have to do it this way!'"

When Wally was called upon to recollect his predecessors, he remembered them all.

Of Grandma Azelia: "She had the most penetrating gaze you ever saw. You knew who was the boss of that clan. Azelia was an exceptional individual. They had a melodeon, which was a pump organ, and a grand piano in the house. She played them both. Of course, in the wintertime they had two things to do—learn music or argue. And they'd spend half the day doing one and half the day doing the other."

Wally spoke from the heart in saying:

"You know, we are a fortunate family in that our early beginnings were two exceptional people."

1. Owner of the *Gazette* at that time.

Maybe the horses are the only ones who failed to enjoy passing through this great tree. L. to R.: Jay Bruce; Al Bruce; Jay's wife, Katherine; Baby Elizabeth; Azelia Bruce; and Eddie Bruce. *(W. Bruce Family Collection.)*

1939. A new generation enjoyed the world's most photogenic tree. Pictured are George Johnsen, Roberta Spelt, Hester Stephan, William (Bucky) Stephan, Danny Johnsen, and Gloria Johnsen—Azelia and Albert's descendants. *(Phillips Family Collection.)*

Epilogue

When he sold his Empire Stables, located in Mariposa, in 1865, John Bruce Jr. left the area, probably to return to Cuba to resume business with his brother, Robert Kale. He died at Puerto Principe on Thursday, August 28, 1884

In 1888, Catherine Bruce Leitch homesteaded 160 acres in Section 35, south of the Albert Bruce homestead. With lumber furnished by Albert, Barnes Van Campen built a house on the property, and it still stands today, a tenacious survivor of its checkered past. At one time, Joe MacKenzie, who had fled France at fourteen to escape military service and subsequently spent much of his life in the area, lived in it. Later, Kitty Bush, daughter of Catherine Leitch, lived in the house. When she moved out, Thornton Jackson, of Tennessee, moved in and squatted there until sometime in the 1930s when the Sedlacheks took up residence. The Sedlacheks added a lot of color by painting flowers on all the trim. In 1946, they sold the property to Ed Vagim, who held on to it until his death. After his wife's death, the National Park Service acquired the house, and despite efforts of county historians desirous of preserving a bit of disappearing Wawona history, plan to tear it down. Its future is not promising.

Fannie Bruce Cook died in 1890. In 1892, her husband, John Jay Cook, published her book of poetry, *Fancy's Etchings*. This was a grand memorial to her.

In 1902, Albert Henry Washburn died, leaving the majority of his stock in the Wawona Hotel Company to his wife and daughter, but it would be John Washburn who eventually took over the management.

By July 21, 1900, when she wrote her brother, Albert, Jean Bruce Washburn was seriously ailing and unable to touch the floor with her feet. She migrated on crutches. Albert had written her of some ideas for a cure, though she perceived a magnetic aura could help. She maintained, "The mind has infinite power if we understand its use." The ligaments of her knees drew up her legs and her hands were twisted. Still in a wheelchair, she died in 1904 at 2525 Fillmore Street in San Francisco.

John Jay Cook died in 1904. Gone was the guiding light which had helped form so many operations. He was spared the suicide of his son, Jay, when the younger Cook shot himself in 1910, after suffering ill health and the disappointment of not being reappointed Yosemite postmaster, a position he had held since 1898.

John Stephen Washburn died in 1917, and the management of the Wawona Hotel was left to his son, Clarence, who ran it until it was sold in 1932. Clarence soon left, moving to Indio, California, where he served as mayor.

When Azelia Van Campen Bruce died, her land was partitioned for her surviving six children. Jay, having debts from his unfortunate sawmill venture, wished to sell his portion. A careful survey showed 20 acres more than originally thought, and each child received 56.748 acres. "It was a survey well worth its price," their lawyer assured them.

In June 1919, Albert Henry Bruce wrote his sister, Jeanette, of his thoughts for the homestead property. "The place has a wonderful future before it. There is a new highway going to be built thru Wawona and people are so numerous—they are camping everywhere. Now we can start a camp here like Camp Curry and in a few years have more money in the bank to the credit of each of us than the place would bring at a sale." Much of the land was eventually acquired by the National Park Service, in separate transactions, as a result of that body's land acquisition policy.

Jeanie Washburn Higgins, daughter of Jean and Henry Washburn, met Charles Higgins when he worked in John Jay Cook's San Francisco drugstore, and they married in March of 1889. They had two children, Charles Jr. and Henrietta. Jeanie was 29 days short of her 76th birthday when she died on April 1, 1944, after an automobile collision in Merced.

Albert Henry Bruce lived in the homestead house after his mother's death. He died on November 15, 1951, and is buried in Merced.

Jeanette Bruce Kilgour Sanchez died in Mariposa on December 16, 1954, after an auto accident.

William Wallace (Willie) Bruce died October 12, 1957. He had given each of his sons, Ed and Wally, a part of his Wawona heritage. Both Ed and Wally lived in Wawona for a time, and later sold their property.

By 1957, Jay Cook Bruce had lost interest in his home, perhaps largely due to the death of his wife, Grace, two years earlier. He moved to Hollister, California where he spent the rest of his life, and there, on February 8, 1963, he died at 81.

Harriet (Hattie) Bruce Spelt Harris's pen was only stilled when, having outlived all her siblings, she died March 2, 1969 in Mariposa. She is buried in Merced.

On October 20, 1978, Yosemite Superintendent Leslie Arnberger informed William Stephan (Jeanette's grandson) of Wawona of a significant happening. The Board of Geographic Names had approved the name Mount Bruce for the peak on Buena Vista Crest. The Bruce historical role in Yosemite history was thus documented as Mt. Surprise was officially called Mount Bruce.

On June 7, 1990, William Wallace Bruce II was invited by the National Park Service to speak of his family at a special Centennial celebration at Wawona. He proudly shared his memories of them to a large assemblage. He lives in Capitola, California.

The homestead house burned down. Nellie Spelt Graham, Hattie's daughter, kept as a memento a melted chunk of what had once been the grand piano. Nellie died June 26, 1996

Azelia Van Campen Bruce was cremated and her urn placed in the Columbarium in San Francisco and later moved to Wawona. On Sunday, September 8, 1996, a granite headstone was placed in Mariposa's Odd Fellows Cemetery, honoring the memory of Albert Olcott and Azelia Van Campen Bruce. It was a tribute made possible by the inspiration of their great-grandson, Thomas Bruce Phillips. Only a few feet away are the graves of both Rose Swaney and James Seale.

Hattie's younger daughter, Roberta Bruce Spelt Phillips, lives today in Mariposa, not too far distant from the origins of much of this story. At Wawona on a parcel of the original Bruce homestead, she maintains a home that her family can enjoy when they yearn for the country life.

Gloria Hope Higbee, who with her mother helped find Allen Kilgour, died August 28, 1997, in Santa Cruz County. To her cousin, Maddalena Gartin, she left the clock presented to her great-grandfather, Albert Bruce.

"Castle on the Green" has long since been replaced. On this site of the ancient Picts, on the corner of High Street and Watergate, another building has succeeded it. R. Hay Robertson operates a shop in it.

A short walk down Wawona's Robin Lane takes anyone in search of history to the area where Azelia and Albert proved up on their homestead by sowing wheat and planting a garden of vegetables. The field is bordered by stands of tall pines. It was doubtlessly once cleared of rocks for easier plowing, but one huge granite boulder still proclaims its dominance as it looms toward the pines.

Adjacent to the home of Charlotte Gibner Train (Johnny Bridle Bruce's granddaughter) is the site of the Bruce Brothers' Sawmill. Nothing is left structurally, but a knowing eye can see evidence of what once took place here. The ground is spongy from layers of sawdust, with vegetation short and stingy above it. Here and there a long rusty nail can be found. Stubs of rotting timber wedge into the earth. Looking upward, a person can see a long section of the hand-riveted water pipe that carried the water, via a flume and water tank, from Chilnualna Falls to the Pelton Wheel which powered the mill. These fragments spark the memory and help write a story fueled from memories.

Wawona's Section 35 is liberally dotted with plots and homes, many due to Hattie Bruce Harris' subdividing. Rental cabins, with handsome stonework, built by both Bill and Wally Bruce, still stand.

Grotto Creek still flows past the site of the homestead house.

Hattie gave her grandson, Russell Graham, Jr. the section boasting Chilnualna Falls. She felt he was the only one who could afford owning the Falls with no profit coming from the ownership. Russell sold his plot, including the path where his grandmother held off trespassers with her shotgun, to the National Park Service. With the proceeds, he bought a ranch outside Carson City, Nevada. He called it the "Chilnualna Ranch."

On July 1, 1998, Chuck Castagna, who resides on Romero Road in Wawona, set the wheels in motion to have that road's name changed to Van Campen Way. Having viewed the temporary display of the Van Campen history, presented by Thomas Bruce Phillips at Wawona's Bassett Memorial Library, he felt strongly that this pioneer family should be honored in this way. The suggestion met the criteria imposed by Mariposa County, and ultimately obtained the approval of both the Wawona Property Owners and the Wawona Planning Committee. The name, Van Campen Way, is scheduled into being in the summer of 1999.

Appendix

ALBERT & AZELIA BRUCE'S
FAMILY TREE

===============

* = Spouse

| Albert O. Bruce 1837-1911 | Azelia Van Campen 1850-1918 |

December 1, 1872
Schlageter Hotel, Mariposa

Elizabeth
1/8/74
Still born in Mariposa

Robert
11/1/75
Died in Belmont, Nevada

Charles
10/22/76
3/17/77
Born E. Belmont Nevada, Died Merced City, Calif.

Albert Henry
1879-1951
*Martha Marian Laird
Albert O.   b. 1906

Jay Cook
1881-1963
*Katherine Fournier
*Grace Campbell
Katherine   b. 1911c
Jay Jr.   b. 1913c
Wilson   b. 1914c
Elizabeth   b. 1915c

Henrietta P.
(Harriet H.)
1884-1969
*James Spelt
*Sam Harris
Nellie F.   b. 1910
Roberta B.   b. 1924

Jeanie F.
(Jeanette)
1886-1954
*Allen Kilgour
*Chapin
*Colburn
*Wheeler
*Sanchez
Alberta   b. 1904
Donald   b. 1906
Hester   b. 1908
Muriel   b. 1910

William W.
1888-1957
*Ada Hall
William W. b. 1916
Edward   b. 1921

Edward W.
1891-1916
Born in Wawona, died on Morvey Hill, S.F.

Robert I.
1895-1924
Born in Wawona, died at Whitcomb Hotel, S.F.

BRUCE FAMILY TREE

* = Spouse

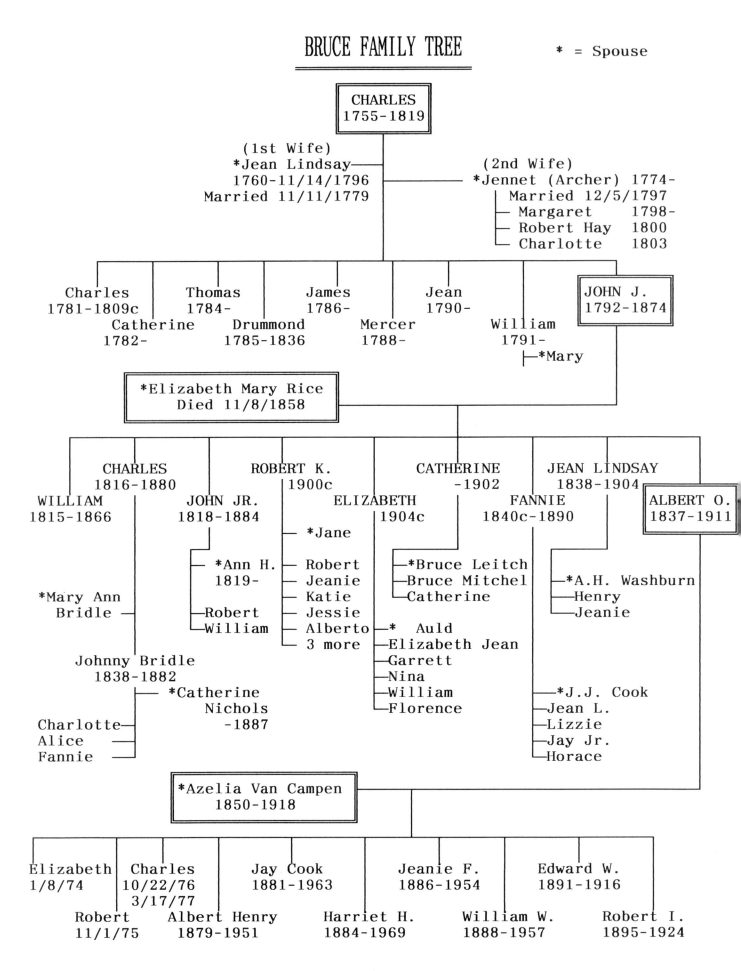

CHARLES
1755-1819

(1st Wife)
*Jean Lindsay
1760-11/14/1796
Married 11/11/1779

(2nd Wife)
*Jennet (Archer) 1774-
Married 12/5/1797
├─ Margaret   1798-
├─ Robert Hay 1800
└─ Charlotte   1803

Charles
1781-1809c

Catherine
1782-

Thomas
1784-

Drummond
1785-1836

James
1786-

Mercer
1788-

Jean
1790-

William
1791-
├─*Mary

JOHN J.
1792-1874

*Elizabeth Mary Rice
Died 11/8/1858

CHARLES
1816-1880

ROBERT K.
1900c

CATHERINE
-1902

JEAN LINDSAY
1838-1904

WILLIAM
1815-1866

JOHN JR.
1818-1884

ELIZABETH
1904c

FANNIE
1840c-1890

ALBERT O.
1837-1911

├─ *Jane

├─ *Ann H.
│   1819-
│
├─Robert
└─William

├─ Robert
├─ Jeanie
├─ Katie
├─ Jessie
├─ Alberto
└─ 3 more

├─*Bruce Leitch
├─Bruce Mitchel
└─Catherine

├─*A.H. Washburn
├─Henry
└─Jeanie

*Mary Ann
Bridle

├─* Auld
├─Elizabeth Jean
├─Garrett
├─Nina
├─William
└─Florence

Johnny Bridle
1838-1882

├─ *Catherine
    Nichols
    -1887

├─*J.J. Cook
├─Jean L.
├─Lizzie
├─Jay Jr.
└─Horace

Charlotte─
Alice ─
Fannie ─

*Azelia Van Campen
1850-1918

Elizabeth
1/8/74

Charles
10/22/76
3/17/77

Jay Cook
1881-1963

Jeanie F.
1886-1954

Edward W.
1891-1916

Robert
11/1/75

Albert Henry
1879-1951

Harriet H.
1884-1969

William W.
1888-1957

Robert I.
1895-1924

Bibliography

Recollections of:
  William Wallace Bruce II.
  Hope Higbee.
  Nellie Spelt Graham.
  Roberta Bruce Phillips.

"The Cougar Hunter," an article in *Adobe Trails,* Spring 1987, by Raymond Petersen.

Mariposa Memories, by Marian Jones Coucher, edited by Shirley Sargent.

The Bruce Family: A History in Letters by Thomas Bruce Phillips and Roberta Bruce Phillips.

A Guide to the Ghost Towns and Mining Camps of Nye County, Nevada by Shawn Hall.

Bodie: Ghost Town Frozen in Time, a Film by Peter Dallas and narrated by Hoyt Axton.

Mariposa Gazette

How the U. S. Cavalry Saved Our National Parks, by H. Duane Hampton.

The Executive Documents of the House of Representatives 1891–1892.

Cougar Killer, by Jay C. Bruce.

Stage to Yosemite, Recollections of Wawona's Albert Gordon, by Annie Reynolds and Albert Gordon.

History: Merced, Stanislaus, Calaveras, Tuolumne, Mariposa Counties.

Public School Registers: Wawona District 1895–1898.

Yosemite Research Library.

Cook Family Bible.

Archival Material of Roberta Bruce Phillips.

Letters dating from 1808 to the 1960s, kept by Bruce family members.

Mariposa Research Library.

Mariposa County Records.

Surprised by the Voice of God, by Jack Deere.

Index

A

Alder Creek (entrance station), 80
American Expeditionary Force, 88
American River, 9
Amos, Joe, 50, 63, 69
Amos Josey, 50
Annex (The), 85
Ashworth, Alice and Tat, 62
Auld, Elizabeth Bruce, 8
Ayres, Thomas, 11

B

Baxter, Ed, 58, 68, 80
Bear Creek Musical Center, 91
Belmont Courthouse, 30
Belmont Mine, 31
Belmont Silver Mining Company, 31
Benson, Captain Harry,
    (Acting Superintendent), 76, 96
Benton Mills, 12
Big Tree Station, 31–32, 37, 45–47, 50, 99
Black's Hotel, 58
Bodie and Benton railway, 36
Bodie, California, 35–37, 50
Bowen, MacNamee & Co., 8
Breuner Meadows, 95
Bridle, Mary Ann
    (Mrs. Charles Bruce), 10, 33
Brinkop, Mr. 85
Bruce Brothers Sawmill, 63
Bruce, Albert Henry (Bert), 46, 49, 63,
    67–70
Bruce, Albert Olcott, 5, 7–8, 24, 26–29,
    31–32, 34–38, 45–58, 61, 65–67,
    70–71, 74, 76, 78–87
Bruce, Alice, 48
Bruce, Azelia Villette Van Campen,
    30–32, 34, 36–38, 45–46, 48–59,
    62, 65–67, 70–71, 74, 76–87
Bruce, Catherine (Kate), 5, 43
Bruce, Catherine
    (Mrs. Johnny Bridle), 45, 56
Bruce, Charles (Son of John J.),
    7, 10, 16, 17, 31, 33,
Bruce, Charles (The elder), 1–2
Bruce, Charles (The younger), 1–2, 27
Bruce, Charles Howard, 34–36
Bruce, Charlotte, 48
Bruce, Drummond, 1–3
Bruce, Edward, 71, 79–81
Bruce, Elizabeth Rice, 5, 7
Bruce, Elizabeth, 5
Bruce, Fannie,
    See Cook, Fannie (Mrs. John Jay), 5–6

Bruce, Fannie,
    (Johnny Bridle's daughter), 48
Bruce, Henrietta Patty or Harriet
    Howard (Hattie), See Spelt, Harris,
    48, 55, 63, 66, 70–71, 74–75, 83,
    86–87
Bruce, Jane, 38, 40
Bruce, Jay Cook, 46, 49, 62–63, 65,
    69–72, 82–83, 90–92, 102
Bruce, Jay Jr., 91–92
Bruce, Jean Frances (Jeanette), 54, 63,
    66, 74, 76, 86, 88, 92, 101–2, 104
Bruce, Jean Lindsay
    (Wife of Charles, the elder), 1, 3
Bruce, Jean Lindsay, See Washburn,
    Jean (Mrs. Albert Henry), 5, 17
Bruce, Jeanie, 40
Bruce, Jennet, 1–2
Bruce, John J., 1, 3–4, 7–9, 11, 18,
    26, 28, 31
Bruce, John Jr., 5, 9, 43
Bruce, Johnny Bridle, 12, 28, 33,
    47, 56, 99
Bruce, Margaret, 1–2
Bruce, Robert H., 1–3
Bruce, Robert Ingersoll, 63, 65, 72, 79,
    82–83, 85–89, 104
Bruce, Robert Kale, 5, 7, 9, 20, 31, 33,
    35, 38–44
Bruce, William (Son of Charles,
    the elder), 1, 3
Bruce, William (Son of John J.), 5, 7,
    10, 20
Bruce, William Wallace (Wally), 11,
    102–4, 87
Bruce, William Wallace (Willie, Bill),
    54, 56, 69, 78–81, 84, 86–87, 89, 104
Bullion Mine, 35
Bunnell, Lafayette Houghton, 11, 17
Burney, Sheriff, 10
Bushhead, Tom, 50, 98

C

California Fish and Game
    Commission, 90–91
Camp A. E. Wood, 70
Camp Chilnualna, 62–63, 93–94
Camp Curry, 72
Camp Merritt, N. J., 87–88
Campbell, Grace
    (Mrs. Jay Cook Bruce), 91–92
Campbell, Marguerite, 104
Castle on the Green, 1
Challenge Saloon, 10
Chilnualna Creek, 72

Chilnualna Falls, 48, 51, 55, 59, 65,
    95–96
Chowchilla Indians, 50
Chowchilla Mountain, 15, 31, 63
Churchill, Winston, 92
Clark and Moore's, 31
Clark, Galen, 13, 15, 31, 40, 48
Clark's Crossing, 31
Clemons, Cyril, 92
Cole, Ben, 19
Conway, John, 65, 100
Cook, Fannie, See Bruce, Fannie, 24, 28,
    35, 37, 45, 47, 99
Cook, Jay Bruce, 58, 75
Cook, John Jay, 8, 14, 18, 20, 58, 75, 99
Coughran, Annie, 63
Crenshaw, George H., 11

D

Deer Glen, 63
Degnan, Daisy, 63, 75
Devil's Gulch, 82
Dewey Trail, 100
Dugger, Richard (The younger), 101
Dugger, Richard, 100–101
Dugger, Tina, 101

E

Eisenhower, Dwight, 92
Elkhorn Ranch, 14–15, 46, 97

F

Fallen Monarch, 68
Fern Grotto, 48, 51, 55
Firth of Clyde, 1
Fish Camp, 83
Fisher & Co. stage Line, 12, 31
Fournier, Katherine, 71
Fourth Cavalry, reference to, 96
Fourth Cavalry, 60–61, 67–68
Franklin flyer, 72
Fremont, John J. C., 12
Ft. McDowell, 85
Fulmer, Elsie, 63
Fulmer, James 63
Fulmer, Malcolm, 63

G

Gallison, Art, 80
General Grant National Park, 91
Gibner, Charlotte Bruce,
    recollections of, 99
Gillispie, Mrs. Bright, 63
Glasscock, A. B., 58
Gordon, Albert, 80

Gordon, Eddie, 68
Gordon, Peter, 12, 16, 19
Gordon, Tom, 65
Graham, Nellie (Spelt), 62, 87, 94
Graham, Russell, 62
Greenock, Scotland, 1
Grub Gulch, 54

H
Hall, Ada, 78–80
Hall, May 79–80
Harris, Harriet Bruce Spelt,
    See Bruce, Harriet, 95, 98
Harris, James Marshall, 95
Harris, Sam, 95
Haskell, Nat, 81
Heald School of Business, 70, 75
Higbee, Hope, 100–101
Higgins, Charlie, 95
Hill, Anna, 63
Hill, Thomas, 66, 68
Homestead Act, Law, 48, 55, 97
Homestead, 55
Hosser, Ella, 50
Howard, C. B., 25
Hubbard, Douglass H., 75, 96, 98
Humphrey, James, 4, 8
Hutchings, Gertrude, 62
Hutchings, James, 11, 17

J
Jackson, Thornton, 63
Johnson, Congressman
    Harold (Bizz), 98
Jones, Lewis Fuller, 12, 22
Jones, Sarah, 12

K
Kilgour, Allen, 74, 76, 100–101
King, Miss, 45, 58
Kinney, Thornton, 63
Kinzer, Amos, 66
Kuchel, Senator Thomas H., 98

L
Laird, Martha Marian (Mrs. Albert
    Henry Bruce), 68, 70
Lamon, James C., 11
Lawrence, Jim, 98
Leavitt, Ernest P., 14, 52
Leidig, Katie, 63
Leitch, Bruce Mitchel Jr., 76
Leitch, Bruce, 5, 8, 30
Leitch, Catherine Bruce, 30, 52, 75
Leonard children, 63
Leonard, Archie, 63, 98

M
Mackie, Frank, 84

Mariposa Battalion, 9–10, 17
Mariposa Board of Supervisors, 23
Mariposa County, 9–10, 15
Mariposa Free Press, 17
Mariposa Gazette, 12, 16–17, 19, 23
Mariposa Grove of Big Trees, 10, 17,
    31, 76, 80
Mariposa Hotel, 79
Mariposa, 8, 10–13, 15–18, 20–22, 24,
    26–28, 31, 53, 70–72, 79
Mark Twain International Society, 92
Marshall, James, 9
May, Harold, 94
May, Norman, 94
May, Patricia, 94
McCabe's Flat, 12
Melones, 80–81
Merriam, Lawrence C., 64
Miami Lodge, 83
Miller, Gloria Hallelujah, 51
Moore, Edwin, 31
Moore, Hulduth, 31
Mountain King Mine, 78, 89
Mt. Gaines, 82
Mt. Raymond, 60, 81
Murphy, Charlie, 63

N
Neal, John H., 19
New Orleans, 2–4
Nichols, Kate, 28

O
Olmsted, Frederick Law, 17

P
Palace Hotel, 29
Pelton Wheel, 72
Phillips, Lester, 97
Phillips, Nathan (Pike), 59, 98
Presidio of San Francisco, 60
Preston, John C., 55

Q
Quillinan, John, 63
Quillinan, Thomas, 63

R
Ralston, William Chapman, 29
Roan, James M., 11
Rochette, Private Chattem, 66
Rodgers, Mose, 8
Russell, Dr. Carl P., 14, 52

S
S. S. North Star, 14
S. S. Uncle Sam, 14
Savage, Major James, 11
Schlageter (Innkeeper), 10, 15, 19

Schlageter's (Hotel), 19, 28, 70, 79
Scott, Myrtle, 62
Seale, Adelia, 21–23, 25, 28, 81
Seale, James, 21, 23
Sentinel Hotel, 58, 75
Sherman, Bob, 83
Snow, Henry, 90
Snow, Sidney, 90–91
South Fork of Merced River, 11, 13
Spelt, A. W., 62–63, 93
Spelt, Hattie, *See* Bruce, Henrietta
    Patty, and Harris,
    Harriet Bruce Spelt, 64
Spelt, James Albert, 76, 85, 89
Spelt, Roberta, (Mrs. Lester Phillips), 64
Stephan, Hester, 100–101
Stevenson, Colonel Archie, 10
Stoneman House, 58
Sugar Pine Mill, 79, 83
Swaney, A. M. (Andrew), 12, 16–17,
    21–23, 26, 81
Swaney, Rose, 21

T
Taber Studio, 75
Tay River, 1
Ten–ei–ya, Chief, 11
Townsley, Forest, 70

V
Van Campen, Azelia Villette,
    See Bruce, Mrs. Albert Olcott, 14–15,
    22, 24–28
Van Campen, Aziel Barnes, 14, 20, 25,
    49, 50
Van Campen, Harriet Angeline
    (Howard), 13, 24–25, 34, 49, 50
Van Campen, Howard, 14, 33–34
Van Campen, Ira, 13–14, 46
Van Campen, John, 25
Van Campen, William, 13–14, 47–48,
    51, 57

W
Washburn, Albert Henry, 14, 18, 30–32,
    35, 47–48, 56, 58, 68, 99
Washburn, Clarence, 63, 77, 83, 85, 98
Washburn, Edward (Ed), 14, 48, 50,
    65, 75
Washburn, Estella, 63
Washburn, Jeannie, 18, 28
Washburn, Jean, *See* Bruce, Jean
    Lindsay, (Mrs. Albert Henry), 18, 24,
    28, 32, 35, 37, 45, 47, 54, 56, 99
Washburn, John Stephen, 48, 63, 82–83,
    96, 98
Washburn, Sarah, 63
Washburn, Seth Caswell, 14
Washington Mine, Mill, 7, 24, 28–30, 46

Wawona Tunnel Tree, 68
Wawona, 40, 47, 50, 52–58, 60, 62–64,
    69, 71, 75, 81, 83, 86, 89, 93, 95,
    97, 99
Weber, (Proprietor of Hotel), 10

Wellman, Eunice, 97
Wellman, Robert S., 65, 97
White House, 62, 94
William H. Spear, 5
Wintermute, Gus, 57, 98

Wood, Captain A. E., 60–61
Wosky, John B., 64

Y

You, Ah, 100